MW00653999

"The swordsman was then aware that among the rest there was a large demon whose nose was not so very long and whose wings were not so apparent. His robes and headdress were arranged properly, and he sat elevated above the others."

—From *The Sermon*, page 105.
(Painting by Tomioka Tessai)

THE DEMON'S SERMON ON THE MARTIAL ARTS

And Other Tales

Issai Chozanshi

Translated by
William Scott Wilson

KODANSHA INTERNATIONAL
Tokyo · New York · London

"For all the schools [of swordsmanship], when it comes to the deepest principle there is only one."

—From *The Sermon*, page 188. (Woodprint of demon giving scroll to samurai, by Yanagawa Juzan)

Distributed in the United States by Kodansha America Inc., and in the United Kingdom and continental Europe by Kodansha Europe Ltd.

Published by Kodansha International Ltd., 17–14 Otowa 1-chome, Bunkyo-ku, Tokyo 112–8652, and Kodansha America, Inc.

First edition, 2006
12 11 10 09 08 07 06   10 9 8 7 6 5 4 3 2 1

Library of Congress Cataloging-in-Publication Data available

www.kodansha-intl.com

This translation is dedicated to
John Allen Whisler

CONTENTS

[The master] acts, but relies on nothing.

Tao Te Ching

Again, the martial arts in this world only
give fine attention to swordsmanship:
teaching ways of handling the sword,
body postures, or hand positions. Can you
understand how to win by these things?

The Book of Five Rings
Miyamoto Musashi

When the doctor
     gives up, the tengu
  is called.

Kawabata Ryu

PREFACE

Japan has always revered the martial arts. In Shinto myth, the very islands that make up the nation are said to have been formed by the heavenly deities, Izanagi and Izanami, with the aid of a single spear. Historically, the differing styles of the martial arts probably began on a very basic level with the divergent groups of people who invaded the islands about twenty-three hundred years ago, carrying with them weapons of varying shapes and materials. Closer to our time, schools of the martial arts began to develop from the late twelfth century, when the samurai conflicts and wars began in earnest, and then proliferated with the Period of Civil Wars during the fifteenth and sixteenth centuries. Eventually, the old Chinese classification of the Eighteen Martial Arts, the *Bugei Juhappan* (武芸十八般),[1] became firmly established. The number eighteen was only a conventional designation, however, and did not accurately enumerate the profusion of schools and weapons that were evolving.

By the early eighteenth century, the aspiring martial artist would have to chose from a confusing array of schools, teachers, and weapons. Different styles or ryu (流) had developed into innumerable sub-styles,[2] with each new teacher to hang out a shingle professing to use techniques that would brook no defense. Some styles taught subtle footwork and postures, some the use of quick changes in position, and others fancy hipwork and tripping techniques. Still others taught subtle breathing cadences, unique ways of holding the sword in order to extend its reach, concentration techniques, and even esoteric Buddhist mantras. The variety of weapons included swords of different lengths (from the very long to the very short), spears with hooks, tubes or other devices, the *jutte*, the *kusarigama*, and various shapes of *shuriken*, to name just a few.

Even earlier, in the mid-seventeenth century, Miyamoto Musashi, arguably the greatest martial artist in the history of Japan, had noted this trend and written:

> When you look at the world, the various arts have been tailored to be items for sale. Likewise, a person thinks of himself as something to be sold, and even the implements of these Ways are proferred as merchandise. This mentality divides the flower and the fruit into two, and makes much less of the fruit than the flower. In this Way of the Martial Arts especially, form is made into ornament, the flower is forced into bloom, and technique is made into display: one talks of this dojo or that dojo, teaching this Way or that Way, in an attempt to gain some benefit.[3]

And,

> Looking into other styles, I have found that they were either speaking with clever pretexts or demonstrating detailed

hand maneuvers; while they looked good to the eye, none of them had the heart of the truth.[4]

"The heart of the truth," and the very essence of heart or mind,[5] is the subject of *The Demon's Sermon on the Martial Arts*, written by Niwa Jurozaemon Tadaaki (1659–1741), a samurai of the Sekiyado fief.[6] Little is known of this man, whose nom de plume was Issai Chozanshi,[7] but he was clearly acquainted with swordsmanship, philosophy, and art, had made an extensive study of Buddhism, Confucianism, Taoism, and Shinto, and seems to have been familiar with the works of Musashi and the priest Takuan. His writings, mostly completed during the second decade of the eighteenth century, are a masterful syncretic treatment of these philosophies and religions, illuminating the central meaning of each, either in direct instructions on the martial arts or in humorous and fanciful stories that instruct in a more circuitous way. His writing style has a corollary in paintings, popular during his time, of the Buddha, Lao Tzu, and Confucius talking together, or tasting wine or vinegar from the same pot: the essence is the same, only the individual perceptions differ. What is important is to understand that essence.

The Demon's Sermon on the Martial Arts offers no advice on techniques, strategies, or maneuvers. Rather, it seeks to set the martial artist firmly on an inward path, a path of non-dependence, spontaneity, and ease. Setting out on this Way—essentially opening up the mind to a very different disposition—the martial artist will no longer be distracted over the comparative efficacy of technique, or the superiority of one school over another. With a new mentality or psychological approach he will transcend such concerns, and this, coupled with the proper channeling of the universal energy *ch'i*, will be radically transformative. In other words, if the student can internalize the essence of all the martial arts, he or she can pursue mastery of any chosen style with confidence and commitment. The goal is not technical proficiency, but transformation.

The demon delivering this sermon is the long-nosed *tengu*, a terrifying but not necessarily malicious half-man, half-bird, reputed since ancient times to be a master of the martial arts with the ability to call upon supernatural powers. Periodic sightings of these creatures, usually deep in the mountains, have been reported until very recent times,[8] when human beings cut down many of their sacred trees and groves.

I have attempted to set the translations in this volume to the classical Japanese rhythm of *jo, ha, kyu*, considered to be the universal rhythm of things by masters of swordsmanship,[9] Noh actors,[10] musicians, and men of Tea. The jo, or Introduction, is a selection of short stories from Chozanshi's *The Hayseed Taoist (Inaka Soshi)*, which offers an unencumbered way of non-attachment and clarity for dealing with the world and its contentions, and provides the proper mental framework with which to proceed to the main body of the work. The ha, or Change, is the author's *The Demon's Sermon on the Martial Arts (Tengu Geijutsuron)*, which applies the above values of non-attachment and clarity to the martial arts, and emphasizes the importance of the primordial essence of mind and of the development and function of ch'i. The kyu, or Impact, is again a story taken from *The Hayseed Taoist—The Mysterious Technique of the Cat (Neko no Myojutsu)*. This has been a perennial favorite of the martial artists of Japan, and it brings the entire work to a tight conclusion and summary.

I have also added in the endnotes a number of references to early Chinese sources, influential to Chozanshi's thoughts, that I found helpful or interesting. For those who do not read Asian languages, but who would like to read further in these sources, I recommend Burton Watson's perennially pleasing translation of Chuang Tzu; John C. Wu's and Red Pine's scholarly and insightful translations of the *Tao Te Ching*, and Simon Leys' new translation of the *Confucian Analects*. It seems to me that Herbert Giles once translated the *Lieh Tzu*, but that work apparently is no longer available. For selections from *Lieh Tzu* as well as the above mentioned works and many others, Wing-tsit Chan's *A Source Book in Chinese Philosophy* is excellent.

With great appreciation, I would like to thank my editor Barry Lancet for patiently and unerringly guiding me through this project; Kuramochi Tetsuo, Senior Editor at Kodansha International, for his encouragement and support; Mike and Diane Skoss for providing me with source materials that would otherwise have been unavailable; Dr. Justin Newman and Dr. Daniel Medvedov for their enlightening comments on some of the more difficult Chinese concepts covered in this work; Robin D. Gill for his astute observations and suggestions concerning my translation of *Meeting of the Gods of Poverty in a Dream*, and for his help in locating haiku on tengu; Ando Ryuji of Kiso-Fukushima, a *nakanori* in the Ontake-kyo (a religion based on the worship of Mt. Ontake) who kindly consented to an interview concerning the practices and meaning of his faith; my wife, Emily, for her constant patience and encouragement; and the snows, trees, and shadows of Mt. Kurama for guiding my passage. Once again, I owe a deep bow of gratitude to my late professors, Dr. Richard McKinnon and Professor Hiraga Noburu, whose memories always make me sit just a little straighter in my chair.

Any and all mistakes are my own.

INTRODUCTION

Background

According to the ancient *Chronicles of Japan*,[1] a large comet appeared over the capital in 637 A.D., the ninth year in the reign of Emperor Jomei. This comet moved across the sky from east to west, making a sound like thunder. Everyone, from the emperor to the commoners, was troubled by this phenomenon and considered it an evil omen. A visiting Chinese scholar, Seng Min, however, declared: "This is not a meteor or falling star. It is a tengu. Its barking voice only resembles the thunder."

Neither the origin nor the appearance of the tengu that astonished Emperor Jomei and his subjects are clear. Although the kanji (天狗) literally mean "heavenly dog," the dictionaries of Emperor Jomei's time defined tengu as an *amatsukitsune*, or "heavenly fox."[2] By the eleventh and twelfth centuries, however, the Japanese people understood tengu to be formless spirits[3] that lived in the mountains, trees, and rocks; soon thereafter they observed that these spirits took the shapes of winged men with the heads of kites.[4]

The tengu of these times could be mischievous, malicious, or even evil. They enjoyed frightening people by creating sudden whirlwinds on calm days, or by pushing down trees; but they could also possess both men and women, causing them to do strange and worrisome things. At their worst, tengu brought about great harm: in the eleventh-century collection of tales, *Konjaku Monogatari*, there is a story of a Buddhist priest being kidnapped (as he relieved himself from the refectory balcony) by a tengu planning to kill the unfortunate man for sport.

With beaked faces, feathered wings, and heavy talons, tengu were fearsome creatures. Terrifyingly quick,[5] they could move from one place to the next almost instantaneously. Shape-shifters, they might have been the shabby old priest encountered on a lonely road or even in the capital. According to the *Taiheiki*,[6] a troupe of traveling actors invited into a castle were secretly observed to be tengu, but disappeared before they could be killed, leaving only the muddy tracks of birds. It is said that foxes—also shape-shifters and miscreants—understand them completely.[7]

By the sixteenth and seventeenth centuries, some tengu had evolved both physically and spiritually, and were now classified into three basic types. The smaller, or *karasu*[8] tengu seemed not to have changed at all, and still performed evil deeds like setting fires and kidnapping children; they were known to feel enmity and anger toward human beings for cutting down the trees where they lived. Their physical attributes were unchanged as well: the same small, beaked faces, wings, and talons of earlier tengu.

The second type was somewhat more evolved, with a more human visage, but was still capable of mischievous deeds. It was this tengu that enjoyed tormenting priests who were either arrogant or who misused supernatural powers. Swordsmen who took advantage of their skills for personal gain or to discomfit others also fell victim to this creature. It was a quick thinker and its talk was often full of confusing Zen phrases.

The most evolved of the tengu, however, were those who sometimes assumed human faces (albeit with long noses,[9] indicating that they suffered from arrogance), and flew with the aid of eight-feathered fans. These tengu became protectors of Buddhism, rewarding good and punishing evil; they were called *konoha*[10] or *yamabushi* tengu. While all tengu had great abilities as swordsmen, it was from the konoha tengu that Minamoto Yoshitsune, Kobayakawa Takakage, and the swordsman in the *Tengu Geijutsuron* learned their art.[11]

How the tengu were able to evolve physically, and to what extent they had evolved spiritually, has always been in dispute. Differing reports on aspects of the tengu may well be owed to the difference in people's perceptions and to the effects of encountering such creatures, with their unsettling appearance, supernatural powers, and quick tempers. People still do not readily enter at night mountains known to be inhabited by tengu, and strange-looking priests wandering alone may be avoided as possibly being tengu in disguise. In April of 1825, the shogun Tokugawa Ienari traveled to Mt. Nikko, and the year before his trip, officials erected eight-foot high signposts throughout the mountain commanding tengu and all other resident demons to temporarily vacate the area while the shogun passed through.

The *konoha* tengu were often seen wearing priest-like clothing, and even became temple guardians. They were experts in Buddhist ascetic practices, which they used to great effect in the martial arts. It is thought that perhaps they learned these mysteries by observing priests who came alone into the mountains to perform the esoteric rituals of *Shugendo*. It is with these priests that tengu are often associated, or with whom they are often confused.

Since ancient times, mountains in Japan have been considered to be the sacred space between this world and the other. The early inhabitants buried their dead in the mountains, and after a certain time the souls of the dead became resident spirits and gods. The rocks, trees, and waters of the mountains, too, were—and still are—believed to be sacred and to harbor divine spirits called *kami*. With the immigration of Koreans and Chinese in the sixth and seventh centuries, mountains were understood to possess a very powerful ch'i—the universal energy flowing through and animating all things—as well. Eventually, certain mountains themselves were identified as gods—supernatural places entered only with trepidation and great respect.

Thus composed of both profane earthly elements and the spiritually sacred, mountains possess a profoundly liminal character, and those who reside there—tengu, other demons, and mountain priests—are seen as sharing that character as well.

By the ninth and tenth centuries, a religion, still very current today, evolved that was based on ascetic practices in the mountains. It is called Shugendo (修験道); literally, the Way of Ascetic Practice and Its Manifestation. A syncretic belief influenced by ancient mountain practices, the native Shinto religion, Taoism, esoteric Buddhism, and perhaps ancient shamanism, its practitioners, called *shugenja* or yamabushi,[12] cultivate techniques of acquiring and manipulating the supernatural forces of the mountains. This they achieve by the worship of certain deities,[13] incantations, the reading of sutras, or other esoteric practices, the most exacting of which is, perhaps, meditating beneath waterfalls[14] in the middle of winter. All of these practices are said to require great fortitude, however. Purifying oneself and developing total concentration are difficult and exhausting matters. Communicating with a deity or actually becoming one with him will bring the practitioner to the point of physical and spiritual exhaustion.

Shugendo's fundamental belief supporting these practices is that the everyday realm of existence is controlled by a separate supernatural realm, and that that supernatural realm can best be entered and participated in through certain rites conducted in the most supernatural of places: deep in the mountains. Shugendo reasons that as a product of the universe, man shares its divine nature and, by cultivating certain practices, can become divine himself. Thus, supernatural powers are available to those who have the knowledge, will, and stamina to obtain them.

It is not hard to imagine that the priests of Shugendo are both respected and feared. As men with supernatural powers, they are sought out for any number of beneficial activities, such as divinations, exorcisms, and ceremonies for avoiding disasters, and for their amulets and charms that ensure safe childbirth, health, and protection from theft. On the other hand, the acquisition of such powers does not guarantee that the possessor will be endowed with good character or be without arrogance and willful behavior. In other words, supernatural powers may be used with either malicious or benign intent.

With this in mind, it is not particularly strange that these priests have been identified with or mistaken for tengu for nearly as long as they have exercised their dangerous powers in the mountains.

As moderns in our urbane, civilized, and mostly deforested world, it is easy for us to dismiss both the tengu and the yamabushi as mere mythology or exaggeration. But perhaps we should not be so quick to do so. Stories of tengu have existed since the early Heian period and are noted in any number written works.[15] Clearly, the Tokugawa shogunate was concerned enough about tengu to temporarily banish them from the shogun's route in the nineteenth century; Ueshiba Morihei, the founder of Aikido, is reported to have learned some of his martial arts from the tengu on Mt. Kurama in the 1920's; and the British anthropologist Carmen Blacker had a hair-raising encounter with someone or something like a tengu as she hiked over that mountain as recently as 1963.[16] As for their religious counterparts, the yamabushi can sometimes still be observed today in their conspicuous outfits on the streets of Kyoto, and they are always given wide berth.

Still, the question arises: have people simply mistaken yamabushi for tengu, or perhaps might it be the other way around? Chozanshi would probably say that this is not really the point. He would more likely declare that the tengu, the yamabushi, and the mountains themselves are symbols or paradigms of what we must become and of the spiritual geography that we must travel. The martial artist in particular must inhabit that same liminal world between the sacred and profane to truly grasp his art. Like the tengu and the yamabushi, he must participate in and understand both this world and the other.

The Demon's Sermon on the Martial Arts

The substance of Chozanshi's work in this volume is first the transformation of the martial artist vis-a-vis mental stance, and the ease or facility of his own body; and secondly how this transformation will be supported, succored and strengthened by the psycho-physiological energy called ch'i.

The subject of transformation is covered in the *Discourses* in short, fanciful stories that require no specialized or heuristic knowledge. The topics of these stories range from the true simplicity of the matter of life and death, one's relation to the phenomena of the world and the very phenomenon of being alive, to the nature of movement and skill and the elimination of desires that obscure the clarity of our vision. At first glance, some of these topics may seem to have little connection with the martial arts, but Chozanshi sees them as fundamental, and untangles them with an adroit and whimsical style.

With an attentive perusal of what may seem to be light and playful stories, the reader will find himself offered a different footing to approach the problems of hostility and conflict. Indeed, he may find that such problems are not what he formerly thought them to be.

In *The Demon's Sermon on the Martial Arts*, Chozanshi turns from transformational insight to the subject of ch'i, the energy that flows through all matter, both organic and inorganic. An understanding of this force and how it affects the world and the individual acting within the world is of vital concern to the martial arts; and requires a more specific vocabulary than that used in the *Discourses*. These terms, indeed, are the lodestars of the demon's sermon.

Ch'i (氣)

The most prominent concept, and the central concern of the demon's sermon, is that of ch'i and its application to the martial arts. Defined variously as "vital energy," "vital power," "universal breath," and "matter-energy," it is understood by Chozanshi to be a material force that constitutes and pervades the universe. To the Taoists it originates in Primordial Emptiness; to Confucianists, Primordial Existence. But whatever its origin, it is the primary energy-substance that expands and contracts, integrates and disintegrates, and by sinking and rising creates and continuously transforms everything in existence.

The original kanji for ch'i was written (氣), resembling the

shape of rising steam, or the exhalation of inspiration of man, transforming itself into air, clouds, steam, and breath. Later, the radical for rice (米) was added, giving the kanji the symbolic sense of the breath, vitality, or spirit that sustains all things.

In early Chinese thought, ch'i is the most fundamental natural phenomenon that transforms and flows; it is the essential substance or thing-in-itself that manifests everything between heaven and earth: light and dark, man and mountain. Ch'i is the foundation, the wellspring of life.

Later philosophers began to see that all physical form, physical energy, and spirit are identical with ch'i, the particular form or energy depending on how heavy or light, opaque or clear that ch'i is. Condensing, it forms solid matter; evaporating, it becomes spirit or potential. Coming together, it manifests itself as life; dispersing, it manifests itself as death. In any manifestation, however, it is a field of energy, spontaneously and continuously in self-transformation.

If the universe itself is ch'i, continuously manifesting itself according to circumstances, it follows that the individual entity of people or things is no more than an illusion, and that birth and death are only events, or even wayfarers, in the constant transformation of this ubiquitous material force. In what must have been an interesting declaration for martial artists, an early Taoist claimed that if you could fully grasp this ongoing process of illusion, you would no longer be obstructed by things; "nothing would be able to attack you; your body will be dark, and you will be able to caress crocodiles and whales."[17]

The implications of these ideas on ch'i in connection with the martial arts are clear in the demon's sermon: we must be able to integrate with the flow and transformation of ch'i; we must be able to ride its changes and understand its manifestations before they ever appear; and when faced with obstacles, we must be adaptable rather than create assertive courses of action. We must take nothing into our minds (or hands) that will come between ourselves and the present event. Ch'i must be free-flowing and neither stiffen nor resist. Thus, the real master "acts, but relies on nothing;"[18] he does not control things, but neither do things impede his way.

To be able to take such a course of action, we are encouraged by Taoists to hear and see with our ch'i rather than with our ears and eyes, and by Chozanshi to develop our ch'i to our fullest ability. This requires some knowledge of the two basic guises of ch'i, and how they transform into the myriad aspects of what we call "reality."

Yin and Yang (陰陽)

The first two primordial modalities of ch'i are the yin—the passive female element—and the yang—the active male force. The kanji for yin (陰) indicates the dark, shaded side of a mountain, where the sun does not shine. By extension, it symbolizes a hidden place or thing, and is representative of the peaceful, soft, stopped, or closed. Yin ch'i is considered to be the fundamental energy of woman, the earth, the descending, and death. The yang (陽), on the other hand, shows the rising sun, the sunny side of a mountain, and the sun itself. It indicates the moving, the hard, the opening. It is considered to be the basic ch'i force of man, heaven, the ascending, and birth.

As yin and yang interact, they in turn give rise to the five ch'i modalities of water, fire, wood, metal, and earth, and from there transform themselves into all of the patterns of the universe. Thus, nothing is inconsequent of yin and yang, and their successive activities make up the universe and, indeed, the Tao or Way. Since all the modalities of ch'i are connected, the process of transformation is continuous and uninterrupted.

This may suggest two important things for the martial artist. The first is that equilibrium is one of the greatest principles by which he or she can act. Going too far with strength or even technique may unsettle one's inward balance or harmony. This is unhealthy at best and a major impediment at the worst. In the *Lieh Tzu* we read:

> The eye will soon begin to squint when it can make out
> > The tip of a hair;
> The ear will soon go deaf when it can hear a gnat fly by.[19]

And in the *Lao Tzu*:

> When weapons are [too] strong, they won't prevail;
> If a tree is [too] strong, it will break.[20]

Thus, the martial artist must keep a balance of yin and yang, the hard and the soft, and the light and the dark.

But the other implication for the martial artist is that nothing is fixed. Nor, indeed, will anything of either solid or more dynamic pattern retain its identity for long. The perceptive martial artist will be constantly aware of this flux, noticing the rise of yang or the fall of yin modalities of ch'i in his or her own dynamic field of energy, and will carefully gauge the balance in time of conflict. Activation of the yin or yang at the appropriate time will be the essence of the art. For the true master, this will not be executed intentionally, but with absolute spontaneity.

With this awareness, transformation or change should be easy, and indeed, the kanji for "change" and "easy" are one and the same: 易.

Tzu jan (自然)

One of the most important concepts in Oriental philosophy, *tzu jan* (Jap., *shizen*), is variously defined as spontaneity, nature, or of-itself-so. The kanji are 自, originally meaning nose, indicating one's self; and 然, now meaning "thus," but anciently meaning "to burn." Thus, 自然 indicated the self-igniting or self-thus. By extension it has come to mean "nature," something existing on its own, having nothing to do with the mind or hand of man. "[It] is done without command, and always spontaneously."[21]

If the martial artist is to cultivate his ch'i and be mindful of the balance of yin and yang, he must move naturally and spontaneously. This means that he or she must perceive any situation with total concentration, and act as a mirror spontaneously reflects what passes in front of it. He can harbor no thoughts of prepared actions, for they will only come between himself and the external circumstances. In the same way, any premeditated action will not truly reflect or respond to the reality of the situation.

Chozanshi agreed with both Taoists and Confucians who felt that Heaven (or nature) is able to move spontaneously because— having no organs—it has no desires. Not having desires, its ch'i is untroubled or un-muddied, and can transform itself into the myriad modalities of yin and yang with ease. Chozanshi and other philosophers went on to reason that a person without desire or greed would have a strong and clear ch'i, and would be equal to Heaven in being spontaneous. Thus, the master or sage would "desire to be non-desiring."[22] Desire means attachment, and attachment can only be extra baggage that gets in the way.

Thus, for the martial artist, context is all-important, and the perception thereof must not be distorted or muddied by anything else in the mind. The yin and yang of a situation must be perceived as they are, and a proper response cannot depend on a preferred choice of techniques.

This way of thinking was shared by Zen monks, for whom self-nature meant precisely spontaneity. As the 7th century Seng Tsan said in his *Hsinhsinming*, "The ultimate Way is not difficult; only avoid picking and choosing."[23] Or, perhaps even more to the point, "Let [your concepts and ideas] go, and you will be spontaneous."[24]

Again, to move with spontaneity, the martial artist must let his ch'i flow by clearing all choices and premeditation from his mind.

Doing so, he will act naturally and appropriately to the circumstances at hand. In a passage with which Chozanshi must have been familiar, the 4th century B.C. Shen-tzu states:

> When birds fly in the air and fish swim in the deep, they do not do so through any conscious art. Therefore, birds and fish do not themselves know that they are capable of flying or swimming; if they knew this, and set their minds on doing it, they would inevitably fall down and be drowned. It is likewise with the moving of man's feet and the grasping of his hand, the listening of his ears, and the seeing of his eyes. At the time of their moving, grasping, hearing, and seeing, these act so of their own accord at the proper occasion, and do not wait for the act of thinking before doing so. If they had to wait for thought before acting, they would become exhausted. Hence, it is those persons who accord themselves with the spontaneous (自然) who long survive, and those who attain to the constant norm who win out.[25]

Wu-wei (無為)

The corollary to spontaneity or the of-itself-so is *wu-wei*, or taking no action. Or, in Lao Tzu's phrase *wei-wu-wei* (為無為): acting without taking action. Just as spontaneity takes place when the ch'i of yin and yang are allowed to flow with natural freedom, taking no action means to go with the flow of conditions or events, and not to force phenomena against their natural bent.

Chuang Tzu expressed it in this way:

> The mind used by the man who has arrived is like a mir-
> ror. He neither sends things off, nor does he go out to
> greet them. He responds to things, but does not keep them.
> Thus he is able to cope with things, but is not bothered by
> them.[26]

For Chozanshi and his approach to the martial arts, wu-wei
means taking no assertive action. In particular, he would not
have the martial artist take any actions that depend on previously
formed ideas or principles that have to be force-fit into the present situation.

When acting with spontaneity or wu-wei, the martial artist
takes up no perspective of his own, but lets his mind mirror the
particular perspective of what is in front of and all around him.
This means responding in accordance with not only his own abilities but also the abilities of his opponent. In this way, if one takes
the course of spontaneity and *wu-wei*, confrontation with even the
strongest opponent becomes a "happy excursion" of "free and
easy wandering." (逍遥遊)[27]

> Being and non-being give birth to each other;
> The difficult and easy mutually come to be.
> The long and short are mutually compared;
> The high and low are mutually disposed.
> Sound and voice mutually conform;
> Front and back follow one after another.

Therefore the sage
> Conducts matters without taking action...
> He acts, but relies on nothing.[28]

Wu-hsin (無心)

Finally, the state of mind that allows free play to spontaneity and taking no action is called *wu-hsin* (Jap., *mushin*), or No-Mind. This is a mind as devoid of distracting thoughts as it is vacant of greed, anger, and ignorance (illusion). Having solved the deceptively great problem of life and death, it is a mind without fear. Completely without preferences or prejudices to get in its way, it is able to act as a mirror to its surroundings and to respond without relying on anything. It is a mind that sees everything as it is, and moves with freedom and ease.

In a letter to the sword master Yagyu Munenori, the Zen priest Takuan discussed No-Mind in this way:

> The No-Mind is the same as the Right Mind. It neither congeals nor fixes itself in one place. It is called No-Mind when the mind has neither discrimination nor thoughts, but wanders about the entire body and extends throughout the entire self.
>
> The No-Mind is placed nowhere, yet it is not like wood or stone. Where there is no stopping place, it is called No-Mind. When it stops, there is something in the mind...
>
> When this No-Mind has been well developed, the mind

does not stop with one thing. It is like water overflowing and exists within itself. It appears appropriately when facing a time of need.

The mind that becomes fixed and stops in one place does not function freely. Similarly, the wheels of a cart go around because they are not rigidly in one place. If they were to stick tight, they would not go around. The mind is also something that does not function if it becomes attached to a single situation.[29]

This is the mind in which ch'i flows easily and harmoniously, in which the yin and yang go through their transformations with spontaneity, and with which the martial artist has the freedom to act without taking action.

In an instructive but deceptively simple statement, Lin-chi (d. 866), the Chinese Zen priest, put it this way:

In Buddhism, it's useless to make great efforts.
Just do with your everyday No-Mind.
Relieve your bowels and empty your bladder,
Wear your clothes, eat your meals, and lie down
    when you're sleepy.[30]

Finally, in the *Mysterious Technique of the Cat*, Chozanshi summarizes his work with the parable of an old, toothless cat, which is, nonetheless, a very effective mouser. In this parable, he encourages the martial artist to rely, not on dexterity, technique, or speed, but on the very way things are, and to follow the nature of the universe. By moving along effortlessly with transformation and change, his actions will be contingent *only* upon what he encounters. Possessing an uncluttered mind with no baggage, he will be free to act appropriately and with ease.

In this short classic, we are repeatedly advised to act by relying on nothing, to do without doing, and to employ the technique of no technique. This is the secret shared by both the demon and the cat. It is the secret that was understood and internalized by only a handful of the most famous swordsmen of Japan.

It is the secret of holding the sword with Nothing in your hands.

THE DISCOURSES

TRANSFORMATION OF THE SPARROW AND THE BUTTERFLY

The sparrow once said to the butterfly, "When I look at you, I can see that in your previous form[1] you were once a caterpillar. Long ago, you tumbled along in the vegetable gardens and were unable to move around freely; but finally you attached yourself to a leaf and wriggled away accordingly. Now you've transformed into a butterfly. You visit the flowers, chase after their fragrances, and have taken on a body that can fly around at will. How pleasant this must be compared with long ago. Now, even though you can say I'm a tiny bird, I do have wings, I have feet, and I can walk and fly as my heart desires. Nevertheless, I have heard a story that in September I'll enter the ocean and become a clam.[2] When I look at clams, I see that they have no eyes or noses, nor do they have hands or feet. They hide in shells and from time to time stick out their tongues, but have no idea what they're eating. They tumble along in the water even when it's terribly cold, and just bury themselves in the sand. What will I do if I turn into such a thing? It would be much better if I had been born a clam, although I would still think it shameful. But having once been born a sparrow with a body that freely enjoyed the mountains and forests, and then changing into a clam and bearing the hardships and bitterness of being in the water, following the ebb and flow of the tides, growing thin, then growing fat—how annoying it would be to yearn for former times. When I anticipate this happening in the future, I can only mourn and be sad. What good karma you must possess to have advanced from a caterpillar, and now to have a body that is so free! And what bad karma I must have to fall from a flying bird, and to become such a different sort of thing!"

As the sparrow shed tears, the butterfly said, "This is not something to bemoan. It's not that you're making a decline. And neither have I advanced. As for concentrating my essence, becoming one thing, and then metamorphosing into another—how could I have a mind to do such a thing? Although I changed from a caterpillar into a butterfly, at the time I had no thoughts about how to make that change. Not only that, but I've completely forgotten about the time I was a caterpillar. Now, when I think about it, I'm sure that I must have lived a life appropriate to a caterpillar. Long ago, Chuang Tzu fluttered about as a butterfly in a dream.[3] In the dream he had taken on the mind of a butterfly and had no idea that he was a man; but waking from the dream, he was once again Chuang Tzu. In fact, he said, 'Did Chuang Tzu become a butterfly in a dream, or has a butterfly now become Chuang Tzu in its dream?' The principle of metamorphosis is just like this. When you make a transformation in September and become a clam, you will move naturally with the ch'i of Heaven and not even be aware that you're entering the sea. At that moment, what kind of mind will you have? When you think about it, it will probably be like getting drunk and falling asleep. After you've become a clam, the sparrow's mind you have now will be completely gone, and you'll naturally have the mind of a clam. You'll make your home in the water even when it's terribly cold, but you won't be cold at all; you'll tumble along with the tides, but will live your life appropriately. It is the consistency of principle that when form changes, the mind and ch'i change with it. Principle has no form, but exists within ch'i. Right now you have the form of a sparrow and, having a sparrow's ch'i, the principle of a sparrow takes on existence. Likewise, when you have the form and ch'i of a clam, the principle of a clam will take on existence. The mind of the form follows that form. When the form is extinguished, the mind of that form disappears, too.

"A long time ago there was an old man. When he was approaching death, a priest from his family temple came by and suggested that he chant the *Nembutsu*.[4] The old man opened his eyes wide and said, 'The ten thousand things are born from Emptiness and return to Emptiness. How can there be a transmigration of souls?' The priest said, 'What can you do when faced with the worst? Just toss principles aside and chant the *Nembutsu*!' The old man shook his head and said, 'Even if there were such a thing as rebirth, it wouldn't be so bad. Honored priest, do you remember the time you were in your mother's womb? What did you feel when you were being born? Tell me!' The priest became angry and said, 'Is there even one person who could remember this? Do *you* remember?' The old man said, 'I don't remember either, nor is there anyone who remembers anything close to the time they were born; much less should there be anyone who remembers a distant former birth. So even if I am reborn into something after this, my present mind will be completely extinguished. Even if I become an ant or a mouse, I'll have the mind of whatever I'm born as and should live appropriately. One life is like a dream, and the next world will also be one life. That, too, will be like a dream, right? If that is so, it is foolish to take great pains at the very interval between lives over something you don't even know. You should die simply thinking, "This is it." That is the best thought you can have at the moment, and is in fact *becoming a Buddha.*[5] With this, the priest withdrew without saying a word.

"Now mountain potatoes metamorphose and become eels; rotten grass metamorphoses and becomes fireflies.[6] Just as an experiment, ask an eel or a firefly if they remember the mind of a mountain potato or of rotten grass. And again, what kind of karma should a mountain potato or rotten grass have? Yin and yang come together and there is form; revolving within that form and its ch'i, there are the functions of motion and rest, and speech and silence. When the vitality is exhausted, it departs from the form, and this is called death. It is because there is vitality in this form that there is a mind with happiness and anger, and likes and dislikes. After this form dies, the vitality is exhausted. In what way could this mind remain? A fire is kindled with burning wood. Once the wood is consumed, the fire goes out on its own. Though there may be some remaining smoke, it cannot stay for long. Though we say that the fire has been extinguished, it will once again be transmitted from a piece of flint. But it is not that the fire that has already been extinguished is coming back from the flint. You should grasp this without saying a word. This is not something you can explain by talking on and on."

THE OWL'S UNDERSTANDING

The hawk said to the owl,[1] "When I look at you, I see that you have a strange shape—a small beak on a round face. Wearing a black hood and a hemp over-robe,[2] you look like a *tengu*[3] from an island of pygmies. Although you have large eyes, you're blind as a bat during the daytime and could not even recognize the orb of the sun. You loiter about and are laughed at by the other birds, but you crouch in the thickets by night, catch half-sleeping little birds and eat them. Sometimes you're used by a bird-hunter as a decoy and are either attached to a pole or tied to a string. This, too, causes the other birds dawdling about nearby to laugh. Miserable bird! Of all the forty-eight kinds of hawks,[4] I think you must be the most pathetic! I break into a sweat just thinking about you."

The owl turned its head and retorted, "Lord hawk, you are greatly mistaken. Between heaven and earth there are those who fly in the sky, those who live in trees, those who run on land, and those who swim in the water. There are those who are beautiful and those who are unpleasant to look at. But each and every one of them received the command of the Creator and was born. It is not as though they had their own choice. If a person could pick physical freedom as he wished, would anyone choose to be handicapped in any way? That I look strange and have eyes that cannot see during the day is the nature allotted to me by Heaven.[5] How could I be exempt from what the Creator has done? Moreover, the long-tailed maggot makes its home in a pile of shit while the pinworm lives in a dust heap, and they think of these places as palaces and towers. A snake has no legs, while the earthworm has no eyes or nose. One can see, however, that they get along quite competently. Each and every thing given birth by the Creator has been granted food and a lodging place that will not cause it problems. To go beyond itself and envy other beings would be turning its back on Heaven. Though my eyes cannot see during the day, they can see quite efficiently with the coming of night. I look for a suitable meal and never go hungry. Although the little birds think I have a strange shape and laugh at me, it's nothing to get mad about. And no matter how much they laugh, it doesn't bother me at all. It's just being laughed at.

"I do no harm to people's habitations like kites and crows, nor am I praised by men like wild geese and mandarin ducks. Neither am I something to be sought out and captured. From time to time I *am* taken by a bird-hunter and attached to a pole and, even though I'm shown to the little birds and laughed at, it's not as though the man bears a grudge against me or hates me. Moreover, it's not as though he's cross-grained or doing something out of mischief; he just does this to attract and catch small birds. It is inevitable that being present in this world involves humility. As for the mouse, when I kill one and am about to eat it, I just sit down to my meal without going to any great lengths. On the other hand, when I don't need a meal, I give the mouse a break and don't go chasing after it. You, sir, are a hawk and, according to your nature, are high-spirited, have beautiful carriage, and are a bird endowed with dignity. You rest on the fist of a feudal lord or someone entitled, and are different from those birds that make up the meals of the common run. Thus, when you go out into the fields, the pains you must take to capture other birds are far more severe than mine. And even if you capture a bird, it is by no means your own. If you encounter a large bird, you could be downed in a fight and unexpectedly poked in the chest by an incompetent veterinarian hawk specialist and thus brought to an untimely death. To have my talons bound and to live in a bird cage would be the same for me.

"Take this single tree. They could cut it down and make half of it into an incense tray, decorate it with lacquer set with gold or silver filigree, and set it in an alcove of an aristocrat or man of high rank as a tasteful ornament. The other half they could make into wooden clogs for stepping through the mud. When you look at the two different shapes, one is admired while the other is considered mean, but they're the same in terms of the cutting down of a living tree."

A nearby bird called the *chogenbo*[6] overheard this conversation. Feeling sorry for the owl, it said, "When I look at you, I cannot say that your shape is elegant, but you have a head, you have a tail, you have wings, you have feet, and you have ears, a nose, and a beak. You are equipped with the entire body of a bird, so we cannot say that you are handicapped. Though your eyes don't see during the day, it is bright enough at night for you to catch fleas. When I look at the many different kinds of birds, the kite is unkempt and full of lice, the spoonbill's beak is nothing like that of other birds, and furthermore, their shapes are disgraceful compared to yours. A quail doesn't have a tail, but the other birds don't laugh at them, they only laugh at you. Are all the other birds jealous, or do they laugh at you because your form is unsightly and your mind lacking in skill although you're still considered one of the forty-eight kinds of hawks? Or perhaps is your current unhappiness because of some bad karma in a former life? Ahh, how pitiful!"

The owl said, "I don't know what the reason is, but even Lao Tzu[7] said, 'There is a reality; men just give it a name.' I can see that there's something strange with me, and that the small birds laugh at it. But this is not something I should abhor. Neither have I become especially pleased that I'm numbered among the forty-eight kinds of hawks. Men have probably named me a hawk because I catch and eat small birds. Yet this is not something I should forcefully decline. It is the owl's appointed task to be laughed at because of men [naming it one of the hawks]. The man who captures me will nurture me. One who is nurtured by man naturally has his work cut out for him. And shouldn't I return the favor just a little?"

THE SEAGULL AND
THE MAYFLY DISCUSS THE TAO

The turtle and the crane[1] were congratulating each other on their longevity and enjoying themselves at the water's edge. A mayfly nearby sighed and said, "Ahh, the spiritual essence of all things, how great it is! It goes round and round, and there's no end to creation and metamorphosis! Among the ten thousand things, it is born and born again. There is growth, there is breaking down; there is prosperity, there is wasting away; there are things that are different, there are things that are the same; there are things that fly, there are things that swim; there are things that move, and those that are at rest. All of the various and multitudinous beings—each tends to its own occupation; all of them tend to the mysteries of their being. You can't see where they came from in the beginning, nor do you know where they go or what they become in the end. I also belong among the ten thousand things and enjoy myself in the midst of creation and change.

"When I look from the point of view of all these many things, I see that fleas, lice, myself, and others like us may be weak little things, but there is nothing under heaven I respect more than us. Is there anyone who would exchange his body for the world?

"Looking at this from the point of view of heaven and earth, there is the great P'eng[2] that beats its wings, creates a whirlwind, and soars ninety thousand *ri*,[3] but it is nothing more than one thing in the great empty sky. It goes without saying that the turtle and crane have the congratulatory long lives of one thousand and ten thousand years, but the length of their time also comes to an end, and the day of their death is no different than ours. Though we are born in the morning and die at night, to me we live out our lives completely. What do the two of you think?"

The turtle and crane had no answer.

A seagull floating by in the ocean heard the mayfly's words and said, "Discussing this from the point of view of phenomenal existence, there are many different things in the world. From the very beginning, this body is formed from the temporary meeting of the four great elements.[4] We come quickly and we leave in haste. Is there anything that remains as it is? It goes without saying that if you want to move around in this irksome, painful[5] world, your body is followed by a hundred troubles, and a thousand anxieties gather in your mind. You simply try to avoid the dust carried by the wind, and live secluded by the rivers and lakes. And when you look at the strangeness of the world's good and evil, you just beg to spend your life in peace."

The mayfly said, "Everybody knows that the ten thousand things are born from the Void and return to the Void. But you receive this body, and from the time you are born to the time you die, for every thing there is a law of nature, and there is an appointed task attached to every form. Those who follow that task and enjoy themselves within it are called gentlemen.[6] Those who

"All of the various and multitudinous beings—each tends to its own occupation; all of them the mysteries of themselves being so."

do not perform their tasks, but instead act willfully, are called lesser men.

"Moreover, happiness, grief, interesting things, absurd things, good and evil, good luck and bad, prosperity and decline, and rise and fall are all created by the Old Man—the Creator—who gives us birth. That you float along in the ocean and live a life of peace does not come from your own resourcefulness. That my life is short is not a matter of my neglecting myself. All of these are instructions from the Old Man. Nevertheless, how could it be that the Old Man loves you and hates me? Every one of us receives our own dispositions and number of days through nature; the Old Man has no understanding of this, and neither do I.

"Heaven carries out its schemes without attachment.[7] And since I receive this body without attachment, and enjoy myself in the midst of creation and metamorphosis without attachment, I should come to my end without attachment as well.

"If, however, you use your own personal wisdom and clever wit, and persist in your own willfulness, you'll be arguing with the Old Man day by day. But the Old Man doesn't give in, and you'll not only torture yourself in vain, but everything you do will turn out wrong beyond expectation, and you'll meet with horrible disasters. If people who are in the dark about this principle sometimes succeed in doing something by their own ingenuity, they understand this to be the norm and, full of pride from their own wisdom and clever wit, labor their bodies and minds exhaustively, and suffer for their entire lives."

PROFIT AND LOSS FOR THE BULBUL
AND THE WREN

The bulbul[1] gathered the small birds together and said, "When you peck away at produce in the vegetable fields or eat berries in the gardens, you raise your voices unnecessarily and make a big noise calling back and forth to your friends. Because of this, men know that you've come and gathered there in a flock, so they spread their nets and put down birdlime. In the winter, when there's no food in the mountains, I come down to men's houses and, though I eat the fruit of the *nanten*[2] at the edge of the verandah, the master of the house knows nothing about it. This is so amusing that I give a loud call of thanks just as I fly away, and return home. If by some chance birdlime has been spread there, I make no noise at all and, drawing myself back, lean quietly backward and hang upside down. That way, the trap remains above, my body is the only thing that falls down, and I secretly fly away. But for you, when birdlime is spread, the bunch of you get all upset, raise a ruckus, and start flapping around. For this reason you get completely covered in birdlime, can't move at all, and get caught. What a blunder!" This he said, quite clearly full of wisdom.

A Jenny wren,[3] a small bird sitting in the farthest seat, laughed and said, "Men are more clever than birds, and once somebody

"A man will learn some skill, and after making doubly sure he's got it down, will use it over and over again in vain, never understanding that that skill has now become his enemy…"

saw that kind of trick, he'd put a narrow trap below as well. Then if you hung upside down and fell to the ground as you said, your back would get stuck to the bottom trap and you'd be in an unexpected fix. So even you, lord bulbul, would get upset, raise a ruckus, get covered with lime, and be caught the same as us. Men of shallow brains in the world are all like the bulbul. Once they achieve something using their own clever wit, they get proud and think they can continue on like that forever. How could anyone in the world be so stupid? A man will learn some skill, and after making doubly sure he's got it down, will use it over and over again in vain, never understanding that that skill has now become his enemy and that he is inviting disaster.[4]

"Long ago in China there was a King Wu who crossed the Yangtse River and climbed up Monkey Mountain. When the monkeys saw this, they scattered and ran away in all four directions. There was one monkey among them that did not flee, but jumped up on a tree limb just like you'd toss up a ball. Demonstrating such skill, he made little of the men below him. King Wu notched an arrow and let it fly, but the monkey grabbed it in flight just like you'd pick something off the ground. Then King Wu gave an order to his retainers, and they all released arrows at once from four directions. The monkey didn't have a thousand arms and couldn't catch them all, so in the end he was pierced through and killed. Those who are proud of their own clever wit and invite disaster are all like this."

THE CENTIPEDE QUESTIONS
THE SNAKE

The centipede questioned the snake, saying, "I move along using a hundred legs, but I still can't go fast. When I'm being chased by human beings, there are times I wish I had wings. When I look at you, I see you have no legs at all, but you move along quite easily. Surely this should be insufficient and you should be handicapped. What technique do you have to move along so easily like this without even a single leg?"

The snake said, "Why should I have a technique? If I simply point my head in the direction in which my mind wants to go, my body follows along. Looking at you, I can see that you go along by moving your many legs. Surely when there are many affairs, the mind is pressed. By what technique do *you* carry your many legs along like this without mixing them all up?"

The centipede said, "It is not that I use my many legs by putting my mind into each one individually. When my Heaven-given faculty moves, then my hundred legs move accordingly and carry my body along as well. Moreover, my mind isn't pressed at all, so what kind of special technique *should* I use?"

An earthworm close by sighed and said, "Well now, men are clear enough about what they've understood, but can't infer one thing from another. The men who lecture on the Four Books and the Six Classics[1] with their magnificent and noble principles, would none of them understand commentary on their own minds. Thus, once separated from their books, they are unable to understand the mind at all. They only listen and memorize, and then interpret the words. How much less could they know *this* mind, *this* body, and the creation and metamorphosis they enter and exit? The centipede's many legs, the snake's lack of legs altogether—both are the Creator's doing and are incomprehensible to the snake and the centipede themselves. Thus, the centipede's many legs give him no adversity; and the snake, with no legs at all, does not find himself handicapped. Now if they were to do something artificial like take the wings from a flying insect and attach them to their own bodies, they would not only be unable to fly but the wings would become obstructions, and they would be unable to walk as well.

"The long legs of the crane and the short legs of the wild duck are both their own natures. If you thought the crane's legs too long and cut them back a good bit, the crane would be in great pain and would die. If you considered the legs of the duck to be short and extended them out a good bit, the duck would be in great pain and would probably not even be able to stand up for some time. This means that even if you improve the legs aesthetically, you would not be leaving a thing to its nature and it would be unable to function.

"For the most part, men may know that there is a function to something, but will not know how to ground themselves in that

The centipede said, "It's not that I use my legs by putting my mind into each one individually. When my Heaven-given faculty moves, then my hundred legs move accordingly..."

function's nature. They know that something works on its own from its very creation, but don't know how to leave it to do so. Thus, they use all sorts of their own wisdom and clever wit, but daily go against the god-given principles of their own creation.

"Look, there are those that reside in trees, those that swim in water, those that lie down in fields, and those that live in holes. Dogs and monkeys alike have four legs, but a monkey climbs up a tree quite easily while a dog can't do that at all. A horse can carry a heavy load and go a long distance, but it can't catch mice like a cat. Each has its own unique genius, which is quite unlike the other's. This is the nature we receive from Heaven. The centipede and the snake have different natures, and their appearances are different, too. The centipede has been provisioned with legs. The snake may not understand the technique for going along freely with no feet, but that's not a problem. Even if the legless snake hears of the centipede's technique for using its hundred legs, there's no way he can put it to use.

"I, too, have no arms or legs, and have no eyes or nose. And even though it's my own body, I have no idea which is my head and which is my tail. I've never really considered this right up to the present, but it's always been enough. If you think this is indeed the way things should be, you will not be compelled to seek things that you would like to know. From time to time I sing a song,[2] but I've never learned exactly what the tune is. Above, I eat lumps of earth; below, I drink from the Yellow Springs;[3] but I seek for nothing in the world. If I'm naturally discovered by a chicken, that's as far as my fate goes. If there's life, there's death.

Why should I be afraid? If you look at it from the point of view of the day they died, P'eng Tsu's[4] eight hundred years and an infant's dying within seven days of its birth are the same. It is foolish to think that all things are not limited by life and death, or that we must have good fortune but not bad.

"Yin and yang, the ch'i that either gives life or kills—all of these are the current of Heaven's Way. I, too, am but one thing within heaven and earth. I'm born in the midst of creation, and within creation I prosper, wither, and disappear. Sunshine or shadow, good or bad fortune—these are the commands of the Creator. How could I dare to avoid what the Creator has done? I just entrust my body to the Creator and don't intrude my own willfulness while I'm here. This is knowing the general drift of the Way."

THE SKILLS OF THE HERON AND THE CROW

A heron and a crow were passing time together. The crow said, "When I look at you, I can see that you have a long neck. You may think that it's quite a prize, but that is not the case. Ordinarily you contract your neck and look like you're shrinking up with cold. It appears as though you only use it to balance yourself when you're flying. Is the length of your neck for taking[1] mudfish?[2] Well it must be awkward down there close to your feet. You must be the origin of the common phrase '*nyoro-nyoro*'.[3] What can you be good for in this world? As for me, if some unfortunate accident is going to occur at someone's home, I go and inform them before it happens.[4] Still, I receive no praise for this; rather, it is considered bad luck when a crow caws, and I am regarded with great aversion. Nothing could equal this kind of ignorance."

The heron said, "That you inform people of impending bad luck and expect some gratitude, and that you're disgusted with their feeling that cawing crows are evil are both mistakes. If you inform someone that he's not virtuous or is on the wrong track, and correct him by pointing out his mistakes, the listener won't believe you. On the contrary, it is men's nature to feel that they're being slandered and to dislike being told they're wrong. When

"That you inform people of impending bad luck and expect some gratitude, and that you're disgusted with their feeling that cawing crows are evil are both mistakes."

I observe what you're always doing, I can see that when you're looking for a mouse, you pluck away at the roofs of people's houses,[5] you peck through and ravage the seedlings and plantings in the fields, you steal the fruit from people's prized trees, and any foodstuffs at all that people have hung out to dry you take and eat without hesitation. This only makes people hate you. Your cawing cries are much noisier than those of other birds, so people's disgust is understandable. Even your informing them of bad luck is not to tell them that they've been virtuous or true, so this makes them feel depressed just like the croaking of tree frogs does.[6]

"It's not that your cawing is the cause of bad luck. It's just that because you have an intuition for ill omens, if there's a house connected with some scandalous event, you feel that deeply, gather around, and caw all over the place. This is a case of 'Similarly pitched voices go well together; people of the same disposition seek each other out.'[7] Why should people feel gratitude for this? And again, are people going to think of you as praiseworthy? For the most part it's not just you, but people are like this as well. Those who feel a boding in their own minds are always happy to inform others of their own coming disaster. Thus, while informing others of such things may be right, people hate and despise it.

"The fact that I'm clumsy is my natural character. Those who go beyond their portion and use their own clever contrivances will always be inviting disaster. It's a common saying that the crow that imitates the cormorant is going to drink [a lot of] water. If I simply abide by my own portion and live my life in foolishness, I can say that I'm following the nature given to me by Heaven."

THE TOAD'S WAY OF THE GODS

There was a man by the name of Bokusai. Hearing that there was a shrine in some province, he set off for a visit. There he saw a man dressed in a dingy outfit prostrated before the front shrine, praying for all he was worth, yammering on in a squeaky sort of voice. Then an ugly old man wearing a rumpled-up light tan cotton robe came out from somewhere behind the shrine and spoke. "Whoever you are, with that cunning expression on your face and the unnatural look in your eye, when I take a good look at you I can see that you're someone with a great desire. You've been praying for something for a long time."

The man in the dirty outfit responded by saying, "How ashamed I am; and how quickly you've seen through to my faults. I am actually a rat advanced in years. Because of my agile nature, it's easier for me to cross over beams and rafters than it is for men to walk along on land. Moreover, I have strong teeth. Because of that, there's no place I set my eyes on that I can't eat my way through, and no place I can't go. Since there's nothing I don't like to eat, there's nothing I *don't* eat. But even though I have this physical freedom, there's this scoundrel called a "cat" they keep in every house, and it's causing me unthinkable harm. My prayer is that, through the might of the gods and buddhas, the cats of this world be kicked to death all at once.

"Listen, the cat has no value in this world at all. First of all it is cruel, it steals fish that have been placed on dishes, it kills and eats the caged birds that people treasure, it leaves its feces scattered around the sunken hearth, and in the end turns into a *nekomata*[1] and harms people. So it causes many disasters and has no benefits. My prayer is not a petition of greed; it's a request for the avoidance of physical harm. An old man, no matter who he is, will make temple visits and increasingly pray for all sorts of things."

The other old man replied, "I am in fact the toad that lives under the verandah, and have no desires concerning the world. I do no harm to people's homes, and so am of no concern to them; if I'm not good-looking, then I'm not lovingly kept in a cage either. As I'm not fond of delicacies, I never think of stealing food. I live in the privy or underneath the verandah, catch and eat the little bugs that fall into my hands, and live my life like this without incident. What sort of wishes should I have that I should pray to the gods?

"A cat causes you injury, so you have good reason to hate it. But take a good look at yourself! A cat is a useless thing in this world, just as you've said. But because it possesses the art of catching *you*, people forgive it for stealing a little food, and in fact put food out for it. It's not that they love cats, it's that they abhor you with a passion. You know that there's nothing valuable about a cat being in the world, but don't know that you're a detriment to society at large. The minds of men of small caliber are all just like this.

"You are naturally nimble and have strong teeth, so you could climb up tall trees and eat their hard nuts; as there's nothing you don't like to eat, you could eat the numerous bugs and crickets in the hills and fields or eat the leftovers people throw on the trash heap. If you did this, would people hate you and keep cats that need so much care? If you had teeth that were just like everyone else's, you would be unable to go into places people protect, you would cause little harm, and people would probably not hate you as much as they do now. It's exactly because of those teeth in which you have so much pride that people are unable to keep you out. It is also why they keep cats, look for the places you live, and catch you. That the clever wit of men of little caliber actually becomes a disaster can be understood from the example of your teeth. Rather than pray to the gods for something impossible because you hate cats, if you reform your mind at this moment and cause no more damage to people's homes, no one will keep useless cats in this world, and your body will be replete.

"But this does not apply just to you. Men do not behave themselves prudently: they blame others and then pray to the gods and beseech the buddhas for things they themselves are not equal to. This is what men of little caliber always do. Listen, the gods do not accept improprieties. Men think that no matter what they pray to the gods for, it will be granted, whether good, evil, correct, or perverse. Men's minds are asinine.

"Look, there is a way to employ the deities. You must first

"Men think that no matter what they pray to the gods for, it will be granted, whether good, evil, correct or perverse. Men's minds are asinine."

remove all selfish desires and distracting ideas from your mind, and so purify yourself within. This is called 'inner purity.' The day that you go to the shrine, bathe and wash your hair, change your clothes, do not eat disgusting things, and so purify your body. This is called 'outer purity.' Cleansed both inwardly and outwardly, when you worship the deity with all the sincerity of your heart, you should drink in a sensation of absolute sincerity as though it had immediately alighted on your head. You should not have disrespect in your heart even for a moment. If you act in this way, you will be influenced by the virtue of the deity's absolute sincerity, and your selfish greed and distracting thoughts will be extinguished; the heart of sincerity will arise within you, and a mind of gratitude will somehow be born in the midst of a refreshing desire to repay that virtue. This mind is exactly the advent of the deity. It is the sensing of the ten thousand virtues and the fulfillment of the ten thousand blessings.

"The Way of the Gods is to respect purity. Thus, the person who employs and celebrates the deity only prays that his own mind becomes more and more pure with the help of the influence of the deity's power. The gods have an unfathomable, wonderful effect, and are the natural form of heaven's principles. If your mind is pure, the deity will come on the principle of 'similarly pitched voices go well together; people of the same disposition seek each other out.'[2] Contaminated by wanton desires and distracting thoughts, you will receive the deity's loathing. For this reason, if your mind is perverse and conversant with many selfish desires, the deity will not come though you pray for a hundred days and a hundred nights. This is like blocking the road and then expecting someone's arrival.

"More than this, you should inquire into the deepest principles of the Way of the Gods. When you look at people who currently try to employ the gods, you can see that they make no efforts to avoid defiling their minds. Instead, they depend on people like Buddhist priests, yamabushi, and Shinto priests, giving them gold, silver, and other valuables to pray to the gods in order to receive happiness, prospering descendents, and long lives with no illnesses. The more extreme of these people promise to make donations or build shrines if their desires are fulfilled, so from the very beginning propose their requests by fixing a price.

"How is the deity going to receive such a man's despicable mind, congratulate his desire, and fulfill his request? This is measuring the deity by one's own base avarice; it is defiling the gods to the extreme. Being struck with immediate punishment is the deity's choosing to 'soften bright light.'[3] If you played the fool like this with someone like your master, he would get very angry and punish you immediately.

"Long ago, a merchant made a request to the governor of his province: 'If you declare that I am the sole supplier of salt in your domain, I'll give you a commission of five hundred silver coins.' The governor of the province was enraged at this request and said, 'That lowlife merchant! If I didn't allow the people in my domain to buy salt from someone else and he alone sold it at a high price, I might receive a commission of five hundred silver coins, but he would make a profit of five thousand. What kind of thing would it be to make difficulties for the people of my domain and then share a profit with that merchant! Don't let men like that in here again.' It is said that with this statement, the intermediary elders and counselors all withdrew in shame.

"This is a well-known fact: even in the secular world it is difficult to use an honest master for the sake of one's own avarice. Needless to say, the gods possess an unfathomable divine virtue. They will only be impressed at your absolute sincerity. Why should they aid the perversity created by your own selfish mind?"

THE GREATEST JOYS OF THE CICADA AND ITS CAST-OFF SHELL

The cicada came down from the tree and said to its cast-off shell,[1] "In the beginning, you and I were one body down in the earth. Now I'll take my leave of you; singing in the treetop, I'll find a nice shady spot and be happy. It's not that I despise you or am tossing you aside. But within my power, there's nothing I can do about you. You should certainly not think ill of me. I will perform memorial rites for your spirit, and will always feel ashamed of our parting."

The empty shell said, "You are extremely confused. Everything between heaven and earth has its own fate, which is not something we have the brains to understand. More than that, though you may sprout wings and sing in a nice shady spot, there is the danger that a crow may come up unexpectedly and eat you. It is the way of the world that if there is joy, there will certainly be sorrow. I now yield up to you mind, spirit, energy, and blood; I will spend my time at great leisure and take joy in tranquility. What else should I require? Without loving life or hating death, I myself will know nothing of good luck or bad fortune, of honor or shame. If I'm blown by the wind, I'll tumble along following the wind; if the wind stops, I'll stop, too, and won't act contrary to things. Even if my form is worn out and my legs broken off, I'll feel no pain;[2] and if I can't do things on my own, I won't have anything under heaven to be anxious or afraid about either.[3] When you reflect on the riches and honors of kings and lords, even they are not worth it. Because I haven't got anything inside of me, I've escaped from the world of pleasure and pain, of gain and loss. Keeping my mouth shut, I comprehend the Buddha's 'bliss of entering Nirvana.'"[4]

The cicada said, "You are truly one who has been delivered.[5] Even though it is said that I drink the dew[6] and seek nothing in the world, I still haven't been able to escape the fact that I'm a living being. It is my deepest desire to hear from you the Way of dealing with this world."

The empty shell said, "I don't know anything about that. Nevertheless, here is something I heard in secret. Creation and metamorphosis give me birth, and I play in their midst. Life and death, good fortune and calamity, are matters of fate. If you love something, you encumber your mind with attachment; if you hate something, you make your mind suffer. To mope about something you're not capable of doing or to lament some knowledge you just can't get is the height of foolishness. Just don't fight with things, and be content with what you encounter. When you don't insert your own selfish will, you acquire the greatest happiness in the world and won't be defeated by things. While you're alive, follow that Way with everything you have; when you die, just be content with your own return. Why should this be so difficult?"

THE DREAM OF THE CUCUMBER

O ut in the countryside in the eastern provinces there lived a
man called Fuzan.[1] He went off to visit a friend, arrived at
the neighboring village, and on his return passed by the bank of
an irrigation ditch. It was the 16th day of the 7th Month,[2] and as
he strolled along intoxicated by the moon, he noticed something
strange floating by. When he picked it up, he noticed that it was
a cucumber[3] fashioned into a horse, with thin noodles for reins.
"Ahh," he thought, "this must have been placed on the spirit shelf
for *Obon* and then tossed away."[4] The shape had been nearly
destroyed, its legs had been broken off, and looking at it made
him a little sad. Fuzan thought that the world was just like this: a
man is elevated and employed yesterday, but forsaken today, and
no one even takes notice of this fact. On the contrary, men are
fools. When given important positions, they display their power
and behave like despots; when abandoned, they are angry and
spiteful and, all alone, are consumed with envy. So although this
horse had just served someone's whim, Fuzan said, "Am I a man
without feelings?" He then packed it up with him and returned
home, then wrote the following down on its belly:

Reins of thin noodles, hemp bones, and hooves,
The beauty of a cucumber used as a dappled horse.
Yesterday you climbed a lotus leaf as a spirit's mount,
Today you are set adrift down a muddy ditch.
Again, we'll make a memorial to pray for the departed.

They made you into a fine shape,
  used you once as a splendid horse.
Then finding you unworthy,
  soon threw you away.
Sprouting leaves in the deep forest,
  bearing nuts and berries in out-of-the-way places.
Can anyone grasp or understand this?
  What a disgrace, no one gets it at all.
Instead, sending vines into gardens and fields,
  they show off their wit and bring about matters of great
  concern.
This is not the fault of Heaven or Man;
  they receive the bit in their mouths of their own accord.
What was first joy
  is later distress;
What started as fat
  finished as thin.
Think for a moment about rise and decline,
  Alone, you'll shed tears of grief.

When he finished writing this, he used the cucumber as a pillow
and went to sleep. Late that night, the cucumber stood up and

remarked, "Everything you said is just the world's vulgar understanding of fame and profit. As for me, I'm born in the midst of creation and metamorphosis, and play in the midst of them as well. I'm not like you people with your stale Confucian thinking. Look, heaven gives birth to things, and gives them each their various shapes and various functions. With a tree you can make a house or fashion utensils; with bamboo you can put together drainboards or make baskets; you can plant things in the earth, mix it and plaster walls, or for things other than these you put it to use according to whether it's fine or coarse.

"From the very beginning, I'm not something praised by man as being elegant or rare. Neither am I something that would be stored away and highly valued by the world. There are a lot of us around, so when it is at last the time of first fruits, you have *momiuri*,[5] *nutaae*,[6] and *namasu no ko*.[7] And for making *narazuke*[8] and dried cucumber, there's nothing else that will do. Green cucumbers are much like us, and as they are made into horses that accompany the spirits of the dead, we're appropriate for that, too.

"But how should I have pride or dejection on account of being so majestically used by man like this? After the Obon Festival is over, there's nothing else I should be used for; so it's a matter of course that, if I'm not needed anymore, I'm set afloat in the irrigation ditch. And why should I consider this an embarrassment or bear ill will toward men? It is my nature to be made of humble matter. Men use various things according to their make-up, and this is a matter of correct content. One cannot hold a grudge against heaven or blame man.

"To begin one's studies with what is close at hand and then advance is the Way of the gentleman. It is my heaven-given nature to be born in a vegetable field. If I unreasonably insist on sprouting vines in the deep mountains and misty valleys and on bearing nuts and berries, I will be willfully turning my back on heaven. But to make one's position replete through willfulness is not the Way of the gentleman.

"Now you consider yourself as having genius of your own accord, you're arrogant to those around you, you see yourself as the measure of what's right and others as the measure of what's wrong. In the end, you don't know how to pass time with the creator of all things. Ahh, you're really a man of small caliber. If people like you are mistakenly put in charge of the country, they will use their own personal knowledge and clever wits, give no thought to people's dispositions, promulgate various laws, exasperate others, exhaust the people, and the end will be nothing but confusion. That you are now of low status and in a humble place is your great good fortune. Leave off this stuff and get on with your studies! Life and death, good and bad fortune, are matters of fate. How can you escape from what creation and metamorphosis have wrought by means of your own clever wit? Just don't bring damage onto yourself by means of existence, or be proud by measuring yourself against it. Comply with the inevitable and know what is enough."

THE GHOST AT THE OLD TEMPLE

There was a fellow by the name of Fuzan.[1] Invited by a friend, he went to pass some time at a mountain temple. The priest at the temple pointed at an ancient burial mound and said, "This is the grave of such-and-such a person who lived in the distant past. This man's influence held sway over the Kanto area,[2] and his martial prowess shone over all the provinces. Now this has become nothing but an old grave, and no one comes to pray for the man's soul."

Fuzan said, "I have heard about this, too. How pitiful! A lifetime of grandeur quickly becomes a dream seen in a garden. Dried up bones in the next world, who would receive any prayers for a thousand years? Our lives, so difficult to rely on, are all like this." He thereupon took a chokehold on his brush and wrote a single four-line ode, offering it before the spirit of the deceased:

Where the flowers of spring bloom, the mountain is like brocade;
When the leaves of autumn fall, the fields rise up in dust.
The grandeur and brilliance of men's lives are all like a dream;
While old tombstones may remain, the passerby wets his
      sleeves in tears.

Before he had even finished praying, something strange appeared from behind the mound. It was neither a woodcutter, nor did it look like a farmer; its hair hanging over its body, it raised up its sleeves and beckoned the two men. "Why are you writing poems and disturbing my spirit? The two of you are carelessly passing judgment on a drab underworld with the minds of living men, and you are greatly mistaken. I suppose you will object, but you should hear me out.

"While I was living, I controlled many great provinces, I was praised by others, and there was no one in the nearby provinces who could rival me. When I left my province and attacked the outside, warriors of adamantine courage protected me from all sides, and there was no place within my gaze that I could not destroy. When I came back to rest in my province, talented and clever men served at my side, manfully expounding on ancient and modern matters. Stringed instruments and voices in song gladdened my ears, beautiful colors brought joy to my eyes, while male and female servants entertained me with their elegant antics. Of the many delicious foods, not one was lacking, and you would think that all the pleasures under heaven were mine.

"Now my days have reached their limit and my life has come to an end; my form has turned to dust and my mind has scattered off aimlessly. I am not crowned by heaven, nor do I step along on the earth. I have no lord above me, nor vassals below. I no longer have the hardship of suppressing enemy provinces when I leave my own, nor do I have to worry about how to govern the people upon my return. I do not have to turn my attention to the beautiful and ugly or the elegant and vulgar, nor does my mind struggle with a thing's good or evil. Receiving the greatest pleasure under heaven, I leisurely return to the Emptiness of the Great Void. Though you may speak of the wealth and honor of kings and lords, they're hardly worth talking about. Why should I take notice that no one has performed a memorial rite for me for a thousand years? Why should I be distressed that no one comes to pray for me?"

Fuzan said, "The orderliness or confusion of the empire, the existence or demise of a province, the glory or shame of one's dependents, the pain and suffering of the masses—not to think of such things is the ultimate inhumanity.[3] Can you consider this the highest pleasure?"

The spirit replied, "You are deeply confused. As for the empire, there is a lord who bears responsibility for it; as there is a lord who bears responsibility for each province, too. Though you say I have descendents, what comes after my separation from life is not within my existence. There is nothing I can do about this, and a person who worries over something he can do nothing about is an extraordinary fool. It goes without saying that the fate of natural metamorphosis is governed by the creator. And though you call someone the lord of a province or the empire, they receive the commands of the creator and then bear that responsibility, so they are just functionaries in the midst of creation and metamorphosis, too.

"To think that a province is something of my own that I can hand down to my descendents forever is foolishness. When the

"Thus, while I'm alive, I do my
very best at my work, love without
selfishness, instruct and govern.
When I die, I'm contented with
my return."

creator changes his command, all my power, technique, and strong-arming will be useless. When creation and metamorphosis dispossess me of my own body and life, there's no begging off. How much more so for a large province or the empire? And we may say something like 'my descendents,' but they're not my own personal heirs. They are the children of the creator.

"Thus, while I'm alive, I do my very best at my work, love without selfishness, instruct, and govern. When I die, I'm contented with my return. I give back both province and descendents to the creator, go into retirement, and should not be even the smallest hindrance. If the creator should give my descendents a province, he will give them one; if he should take one away, he'll take it away. I leave the responsibility for reward and punishment with the creator.

"Right now, you and I are separated by life. The stagnant Confucianism of people like you will put no faith in what I say. But the person who simply knows the unity of life and death, of longevity and demise, and gets to the bottom of it, will understand this in silence." He thereupon wrote a single four-line ode, and was gone:

> One's life, from the beginning, is lonely and desolate;
> After death, you are inactive[4] of your own.
> Look quietly at the world of men—
> Whether they flourish or fade, it's all one grave.

MEETING THE GODS OF POVERTY
IN A DREAM

There was a fellow by the name of Mukyusai, who was abjectly poor. He always put his faith in Daikokuten[1] and prayed for good luck, but there was never any indication that this was working. One night in a dream, he had no idea where he was, but there were the Seven Gods of Good Fortune[2] gathered together with blue, yellow, and vermilion tapestries spread about, gold and silver sake bottles, unglazed earthen cups, trying out various kinds of wine and side-dishes, singing and dancing to thirteen-string zithers, assembling male and female entertainers, and indulging in all sorts of refined amusements. Moreover, when he looked off to the side, there were some miserably thin and worn-out fellows wearing ragged clothes and looking like beggars. Grasping at the dregs of tofu, they ate what they could and sat listening to the others enviously.

From among this group, five or six men moved away from the others, sat down on the edge of a boulder, washed their feet in a clear stream, slapped their thighs, and sang. Then, taking up bamboo flutes,[3] they played away with their minds at ease. The timbre of the flutes was quiet and calm, without a hint of envy and, contrary to what might have been expected, seemed richer than all the amusements of the Seven Gods of Good Fortune.

Mukyusai thought this was strange. He drew near them and said, "Whatever kind of gentlemen you may be, you have a shabby appearance. Yet even in front of the extraordinary beauty of the exalted Seven Gods of Good Fortune, you show no reserve, but deliberately gather and entertain yourselves with elegance."

The men replied, "What quick perception! Such a mentality is the very foundation of enlightenment. When you're not receptive, even though you have eyes to see and ears to hear, you could lodge with Yao, Shun,[4] and Confucius and still make no progress in the Way. We are the gods of poverty, but why should we be ashamed in front of those gods of good fortune? We and they, all of us, have our own fates. Not only that, but while they are on friendly terms with emperors, aristocrats, feudal lords, the privileged class and, yes, wealthy townspeople, and provide them with different kinds of luxury and splendor, they're not intimate with men of virtue at all. Now even though we look this way, in China we were on familiar terms with men like Ch'ao Fu and Hsu Yu and, among the Confucians, Yen Yuan, Min Tze Ch'ien, and Yuan Hsien.[5] We know the pleasures of a split bamboo bowl, a gourd for a plate, and a narrow lane,[6] and would not exchange them for the wealth and honor of kings and lords. For this reason, though those gods drape themselves in brocade, eat fine delicacies, and go through the length and breadth of worldly pleasures, such things are hardly worth a straw.

"Your poverty is your bit of fate. No matter how much faith you put in Daikoku or how much you pray to the Seven Gods of Good Fortune, they are unable to get on friendly terms with you, for this is something that Heaven will not sanction. And what Heaven will not sanction, they cannot be at liberty with. Your offerings of boiled rice and red beans[7] only add to your woes. Those who are on friendly terms with you both day and night are the gods of poverty that look like hungry ghosts in that crowd over there. And it's not that they come here from another place to haunt you. When you were born, they accompanied you from inside your mother's womb. So even if you tried to scrape them off, they could not withdraw; and even if you tried to beat them to death, they couldn't die. This is just the turn of Fortune's Wheel. But if you will understand this principle, let it sink deep into your mind, settle yourself in your dire poverty, and not lose its pleasures; the gods of poverty will be joyful along with you, and there will be no reason to be shamed by the Seven Gods of Good Fortune. Because we were on such friendly terms with men like Ch'ao Fu, Hsu Yu, Yen Tze, Min Tze, and Yuan Hsien, we were transformed and even now haven't lost that joy." So saying, they again slapped their thighs and amused himself in song.

Mukyusai was astonished and said, "This is truly a lesson hard to come by. But I have no idea about that kind of pleasure. I would like to ask you to set forth that Way to me."

The gods of poverty said, "Long ago, Lord Ou Yang[9] said, 'There are many people who are unable to obtain the Most Beautiful and the Greatest Happiness at the same time.' Now what is the Most Beautiful? To live with riches and honor, to possess much gold, silver, and material wealth, to have the finest dress and food, to be in the warm favor of one's superiors, to have a wealth of power and prestige, and to have everything you wish for: this is what the human mind considers to be success, and so is envied by all the world.

"Then what is the Greatest Happiness? To be without desire and to know what is enough, to be perfectly fair and selfless, not to fight about what is right and wrong with things, to understand the very foundation of one's mind, not to be confused by life and death or good fortune and calamity, to entrust life to life and to exert all of your powers in following that Way, and to entrust death to death and to be content in that return. Not to envy wealth and honor, not to loath poverty and low birth, not to be obsessed by thoughts of the differences between happiness and anger or likes and dislikes, but rather following good and bad fortune, or prosperity and decline as one meets them, and calmly enjoying oneself in the midst of creation and change: This is the Greatest Happiness under heaven.

"I envelope the universe by means of my mind; and by means of the universe, there is nothing that obstructs my mind. Riches and honor, good luck and calamity are elsewhere. When you seek after such things, you may obtain them or you may not—this is not something that is guaranteed. The Greatest Happiness is within yourself. If you seek your mind wholeheartedly, you will obtain it for sure. Simply, do not seek after illusion.

"Confucius said, 'Is human-heartedness[10] so far away? If I seek human-heartedness, it is right here.' Human-heartedness is nothing other than the Greatest Happiness. When you pursue things, are unable to obtain them, and yet persist in desiring them, you merely torment yourself. You exhaust your life because of 'things,' and will not know contentment. If you pursue fame, you will be exhausted for the sake of a name; if you pursue gold and silver, you will be exhausted for the sake of gold and silver; if you pursue utensils and furnishings, you will be exhausted for the sake of utensils and furnishings; for those who love the sensual, they will be exhausted for the sake of the sensual; and those who don't realize that they are making their precious minds slaves to other things, will use their minds like this and exert themselves to the very end of the day. Nowadays people call men who are skillful in such matters wise. In the past they called them fools and men of little caliber.

"When you use your mind in this way, you get farther from the Greatest Happiness day by day. But the man who has even a glimpse of the region of the Greatest Happiness has no mind to pursue riches and honor, or good fortune and happiness. The wise men and men of noble character in the past who were wealthy and exalted were rare. From time to time there were men who received high rank and large stipends, but they did not pursue such things themselves; because the genius and virtues of these men were not hidden, they were promoted by their superiors, and thus only received these things unavoidably. But because they were not always in tune with the minds of men of little caliber, many of them were slandered and driven away. This was not unusual in either China or Japan. And although we say they were 'driven away,' in terms of their own Greatest Happiness they were not hindered in the least. Thus, when meeting such circumstances, tossing away wealth, honor, prosperity, and stipend was like throwing away broken straw boots. This was because what they treasured was within themselves rather than within wealth, honor, prosperity, and stipend. Wise men know that such things are fetters and bonds, and there were many men who took their leave and did not receive them even though they were offered. Hsu Yu, Yen Tze-lu,[11] and, among the Confucians, Yen Yuan, Min Tze-ch'ien, and Ch'i Chang-k'ai[12] were of this sort."

THE SERMON

PREFACE

For the most part, in performing techniques in the art of swordsmanship, it is considered essential to develop the body's skill
through patterned exercises with the sword. Thus, all schools
of swordsmanship nearly fall all over themselves in establishing strategies and patterns in great varieties. But when you think
about it, when the body is well regulated, you will already know
the function of change. Relying on the operations of form, and
following the activity and inactivity of change, you will be aware
of the preparedness or lack of preparedness of both yourself and
your opponent. And if your own mind is correct, you will know
on your own the signs of victory or defeat that are not yet apparent to others. Still, what are called the "Death-dealing sword' and
the "Life-giving sword"[1] can by no means be discussed in terms of
form. When the mind, feet, and hands are able to respond to the
laws of change, then the grip on life and death is in your control,
not your opponent's.

Nevertheless, in recent times many gentlemen have been cel-
ebrated in the world because of their swordsmanship. One style
is divided into ten thousand styles, and instructors teach their disciples, one blindly following the other. Some lead their students

on by teaching far-fetched principles, saying that if they study these things well, they will be able to rule Heaven, Earth, and the country. Others teach their students to manipulate their swords to the left and right, to the fore and to the rear, telling them that in doing so, one man will be able to oppose ten. Still others say that if the mind and ch'i are refined and made correct, when confronted one can without a doubt be victorious without even getting up from one's seat. What a lot of braying and crowing! All of these teachings are extravagant and partial, and are certainly not the correct art of swordsmanship. Those who study such stuff receive and pass on these misconceptions, teaching their own disciples accordingly. As the common saying goes, if one dog howls a falsehood, ten thousand dogs will pass it on as truth. Is this not to be lamented altogether?

For this reason, there are not a few who either lose the very crux of the matter, torment themselves with physical techniques, or labor over the art of training the mind.

At this time we are fortunate to have a man called Issai Chozan-shi, who has year after year entrusted his mind to the realm of the sages and the saints, and labored his thoughts in the forests of the martial arts. Moreover, he laments that those who study swordsmanship these days have lost sight of its fundamentals, chase after its trivialities, muddy its truths, and mistake its true principles altogether. He has bound within one cover *The Demon's Sermon on the Martial Arts*, and conferred it upon those who are young or still in the dark. At first, using the pretext of the eerie voice of a demon, he speaks of the true principles of swordsmanship.

In the end he discusses the deepest truths of the martial arts, horsemanship, and all the arts. Finally, he returns to a sermon on cultivating the mind and ch'i. He truly leads the samurai to knowledge of the essential Way.

The book is thorough: going from the shallow to the deep and from the low to the high, it records the network of Heaven and Earth. When a man who would be a warrior relies on these teachings, studies the martial traditions, and learns the sword, he will likely never desire to stray again.

Written by the hermit,
Kanda Hakuryushi[2]
East Musashi, Edo, Toshima District

13th Year of Kyoho (1728)
On an auspicious day of the
12th Lunar Month

THE DEMON'S SERMON ON THE MARTIAL ARTS

THE GIST

Man is a moving being.[3] If he does not move to what is good, he will surely move to what is not. If this consciousness does not arise here, another consciousness will arise there. Man's mind goes through multifarious changes and never stops. If one is not deeply resolved and does not intently study the mind,[4] he will never become enlightened to the essence of his own mind. Nor will he be able to directly follow his own nature, that decreed by Heaven.

Therefore, the sages taught the beginning student only the Six Arts,[5] and first made him into a vessel. From this point, he would discipline himself and aim to search out a transmission of the Great Way. From the time of a man's youth when he studied the Six Arts, the mind was considered fundamental,[6] and a base liking for words was put at a distance. The mind was not indulged with playthings or vacuous entertainments, and the body was not endangered with recklessness and depravity. On the outside, the bones and sinews were strengthened and disease was kept in check; on the inside, the provisions of the state were established, and its prosperity was not taken lightly. When a man reached this point and made clear the study of the mind, he became an aid to the Great Way.[7]

Though one art may seem trivial, one should not take it lightly. But again, do not make the mistake of considering that art to be the Way.

CHAPTER 1

Once there was a swordsman who, pondering his situation, thought to himself: "There is a story that, long ago, when Minamoto Yoshitsune was still called Ushiwakamaru,[8] he went deep into Mt. Kurama,[9] where he met with demons both large and small, and learned the deepest secrets of swordsmanship. Later, he met the bandit chief Kumasaka[10] at the Akasaka post town in the province of Mino, single-handedly routed a large company of evil brigands, and killed Kumasaka. Now I've been deeply resolved in this Way and have practiced for many years. Still, I have not yet learned its deepest secrets or got to the heart of it. I, too, should go into the mountains, meet with the demons, and carry on the highest laws of this Way."

So at midnight he went deep into the mountains, sat on a rock, meditated deeply, and called for the demons over and over. But even though he did this night after night, there was no answer. Then one night a wind rose up in the mountains, and from time to time a strange atmosphere would fill the air. Numerous creatures with strange shapes bearing long noses and red faces appeared in the clouds exchanging blows, their voices heard in great shouts and cries.

So at midnight he went deep into the mountains, sat on a rock,
meditated deeply, and called for the demons over and over.

After a while, they all settled in the branches of a cedar tree and one of them said, "There is no form to principle, and principle's function manifests itself according to the vessel. If there is no vessel, you will not see the principle.[11] The mysterious function of the Great Ultimate[12] is manifested according to the changes of yin and yang. The principles of Heaven in man's mind are manifested according to the circumstances of the Four Fundamental Virtues.[13] Swordsmanship is a matter of victory or defeat. Nevertheless, extended to its ultimate law, it is nothing other than the mysterious function of the very nature of the essence of the mind. Still, it is difficult for the beginning student to arrive at this suddenly. For this reason, the teaching of the men of old followed the self-nature of form and thoroughly covered technique in every way possible. But they applied them gently and without violence. Thus the students corrected the structures of their sinews and bones, practiced the movements of their arms and legs, only grasping the function of their techniques and responding to changes.

"If you have not acquired skill in technique, your mind may be strong, but you will be unable to respond with its function. Technique is cultivated by means of ch'i, and ch'i uses the mind as a vehicle to put form into use. For this reason it is considered essential that ch'i is active and does not stay in one place, that it is strong and robust and is in no way deterred.

"The highest principles are contained within techniques and follow the self-nature of the utensil. As you become skillful in technique, ch'i harmonizes and the principle of the place that contains that ch'i is manifested on its own. When this has completely penetrated the mind and no more doubts remain, technique and principle become one, ch'i is under control, your spirit is settled, and practical application is completely unobstructed. This was the way of training[14] in the martial arts in the past. Thus, in the martial arts, drill and discipline are considered essential. If your technique has not become mature, ch'i will not become harmonized and form will not follow. When the mind and form become two, you will be unable to act with freedom."

Again, one of the demons spoke, "A sword is something for cutting, and a spear is something for thrusting. What could they be used for beyond this? Listen, form follows ch'i, and ch'i follows the mind. When the mind does not move, there is no movement of ch'i; when the mind is at peace and there is nothing to agitate it, the ch'i is also in harmony, follows the mind, and technique responds to circumstances naturally. When there is something in the mind, ch'i is obstructed and the arms and legs cannot respond with their function. When the mind resides in technique, ch'i is hindered and is not in harmony. When you insert strength into the mind, it leaves a fissure in its wake and is—on the contrary— weak. When you arouse intention for controlling a situation, it is like blowing into a fire and using up all the kindling. When ch'i initiates, it dries up; when you fix it, it freezes. When you wait to defend yourself and intend to respond to your opponent's actions, you are withholding action, obstructing yourself on your own, and will be unable to advance a single step. On the contrary, your opponent will simply play with you. If you have a poor understanding of such things as 'Abiding in the midst of Attack' and 'Attacking in the midst of Abidance,'[15] you introduce intention and will suffer great harm.

"There are a great many people who, while intending to put up a stout defense when meeting a strong but unskillful man, are soundly beaten, and are unable to commence an attack with the sword they have. This is all because they introduce intention. This unskillful man may not know the actions of practical application, may not intend to strike at one's defense, but has no fear because he was born naturally strong. Because he thinks of people as being less than insects, he does not intentionally put strength into his actions; he neither freezes nor tightens up, nor does he wait or retreat. Having no doubts, he does not move, but simply faces his opponent without any thought or consideration. Neither his mind nor his ch'i are hindered. His level of ch'i is at a place where it can overcome others far more than that of what the world generally calls 'martial artists.'

"Nevertheless, this is not something to be considered good. Even though this person is as unhindered as the force of an advancing flood, his force is blind and mindless, relying on hot blood.

"Swordsmanship is the practical application of the self-nature of the essence of the mind. Coming, it has no form; going, it leaves no trace. Something that has form and aspect does not have the mysterious function of the spontaneity. Only when it is introduced into one's thoughts is there form to ch'i. Your opponent then strikes at the place where that form appears. When there is nothing in your mind, your ch'i is in harmony and tranquil. When your ch'i is in harmony and tranquil, it will be active and flowing, but it has no fixed form; and without using strength, it will be naturally strong.

"Martial artists today do not know the practical application of the unmoving essence of mind and unobstructed freedom. Using conscious skill, they squander their spirit on trivial techniques. And with this, they think that they are fully comprehending the martial arts. Thus, they are unable to understand other martial arts. Nevertheless, the martial arts are manifold; if you disciplined yourself in them one by one, you could spend your entire life doing so, but never understand them all. Know that you should use your mind well, penetrating just one of them and leaving the others alone."

Yet another demon said, "That swords are instruments of cutting and spears instruments of thrusting is a matter of course. Nevertheless, there are people who go too far in this principle and do not know the use of technique. There are techniques for cutting into the cutting and techniques for thrusting into the thrusting. When you don't know the use of a technique, your response to things will be off-kilter. Though your mind is strong, when you turn your back on form, you will hit a point where you likely won't hit anything at all. When principle runs counter to technique, you will not attain what you should. It's like when people say, 'Choose it, and it's not so bright and shiny; talk about it, and it doesn't make as much sense.'[16] Just because you think a Zen monk is enlightened about the essence of mind, would you give him the reins of government and make him one of your generals? What would be the merit in that? Though his mind has no share of dust, cares, and illusion, he will be useless because his technique lacks maturity.

"Look, anyone knows how to draw back a bow and release an arrow. But if you're not grounded in that Way,[17] your technique will have no skill. When you draw back the bow indiscriminately and let the arrow fly, you will neither be able to hit the target well, nor sink your arrow into it with any force. Your intention must be absolutely exact, your form correct, and your ch'i must fill your entire body and be alive. You must not be contrary to the character of the bow, and you and the bow must become one. When it seems as though your spirit fills Heaven and Earth, you draw the bow and the distance between arrow and target is filled like an empty shell, your spirit will be settled, your thoughts will not move, your mind will assume No-Mind, and you let the arrow fly. After releasing the arrow, you will be all the more your fundamental self. After hitting the object, peacefully put the bow away. This is the practice of the Way of Archery. If you practice in this Way, you will send the arrow a great distance and penetrate the target with force. Bow and arrow are made of wood and bamboo. But when your spirit becomes one with them, there will be spirit in the bow as well, and its mystery will be the same.

"This is not something that can be gained by conscious ready wit. Although you may have researched its principle beforehand, if it has not penetrated your mind, if the technique has not matured, and if you have not piled up great effort upon effort into training, you will not be able to grasp its mystery. If your intention is not true on the inside and your body not correct on the outside, the frame of your sinews and bones will not be solid. If your ch'i does not fill your entire body, you will be unable to endure pulling with strength for long. To have your spirit unsettled and your ch'i stagnant, to use your own conscious ready wit, is not to be grounded in this Way.

"When you use strength to control your pull of the bowstring, you run counter to the character of the bow, you and the bow are in opposition and become two. When your spirit does not pass back and forth between you and the bow, you will actually obstruct the strength of the bow, and strip away its force. Thus you will be unable to send the arrow far or to penetrate the target with force."

The demon continued, "Everyday human affairs are just like this. If your intention is not true and you conduct yourself incorrectly, you will lack diligence in the affairs of your lord and be disloyal, you will dither around with the affairs of your parents and show no filial piety, and not be sincere to your relatives and friends. People will despise you, society will detest you, and you will be unable to cope with things. When your ch'i does not fill your entire body, inwardly you will be prone to sickness and your mind will be hard up; in your affairs you will be preoccupied and anxious, and you will be unable to undertake any noble enterprise. When you obstruct the character of things, you run counter to human nature, distance yourself from matters, and are out of harmony; and when this happens, you end up in conflict. When your spirit is unsettled, you have many doubts and your affairs are unending. When your thoughts are moving, you have no tranquility and make a multitude of mistakes."

The demon spoke further, "To say that there is no movement of ch'i when the mind doesn't move and that technique will follow naturally is really only an explanation expressing the standard rather than the very foundation of the essence of principle. This is not to say that disciplining oneself in technique is a waste of one's resources. Principle is explained from the top down, while training is sought after from the bottom up, and this is just the way things are.

"Man's mind, too, is not without the good. When you follow your own true character and are not a slave to your passions and desires, your spirit will not be troubled, you will be in touch with the phenomena of this world, and practical application will have no obstacles. For this reason, the 'Way of the Great Learning[18] is in making clear your adamantine character,' and in the Doctrine of the Mean[19] it says that 'Complying with your character is called following the Way.' In explaining this great fundamental principle from the top, scholars express its standard. Neverthe-less, the mediocrity and confusion of some people are deep, and such people are unable to change the substance of their ch'i and directly return to the spirit of their true character. For this reason, scholars preach about 'the extension of knowledge' and 'making one's will and heart sincere.'[20] They also expound self-examina-tion and being watchful over ourselves when we are alone,[21] and would have us step over the true ground of self-discipline.

"Swordsmanship is also like this. Facing your opponent, you forget about life, forget about death, forget about your opponent, and forget about yourself.[22] Your thoughts do not move and you create no intentions. When you are in a state of No-Mind and leave everything to your natural perceptions, metamorphosis and change will be conducted with absolute freedom, and practical application will have no obstacles. When in the midst of a great number of opponents, you will cut and thrust before and behind, and to the left and right. And even if your body is smashed to bits, your ch'i will be under control and your spirit settled, you will suffer no changes at all, and you will be as correct and peerless as Tzu Lu.[23]

"If you will be like this, how could you fail or be without result? This is the deepest principle of swordsmanship. Nevertheless, it is not a Way you can climb up directly without incurring traveling expenses. If you do not try out your techniques, temper your ch'i, train your mind, or make intense and diligent efforts without fail, you will never reach this Way. If you are led in your early studies by what my colleague has said, you will become stubborn and vacuous, and will think that you 'have it' when there is nothing in your mind. Becoming indolent, you will be mistaken about harmony and enlightenment.

"The strong, unskillful man that my colleague spoke about bears a resemblance to the kind of crushing martial art in every style, but he is slightly different. Such a man is inconstant and unsettled. 'Defeat' here is using brute force and vigorous strength, and trampling the opponent underfoot. His ardor does not shrink, and he is not perplexed by empty show. Aiming wholeheartedly at the main camp of the enemy, he cuts his way through like a tumbling boulder. Nevertheless, when he is violent, his ch'i is overflowing and scattered, and if he meets up with a man skillful in technique, he will fall into the man's strategy. When you do not know the advantages and disadvantages of form, you will make mistakes. Thus, there are lessons to be found in form as well. In defense, you will not lose yourself; your ch'i will neither congeal nor constrict; you will forget about life and death, and will advance without doubts.

"There is crushing by means of ch'i, and destruction by means of mind. Together, these two become one. If mind and ch'i do not become one, there can be no crushing. This is an excellent initiation for the beginning student of swordsmanship. But when ch'i wavers and there is doubt, he will not be able to put technique into action. There is self-discipline in ch'i, and there is great effort in becoming free from doubt in the mind. Nevertheless, if ch'i takes form just once, there will be no mysterious technique of the application of the essence of mind without obstacle and in complete freedom. If you make a detailed effort concerning this point, continuously strive to understand its principle and calm your ardor, your technique will mature and you will reach the substance of the thing itself. But if from the very beginning you only make ineffective efforts, you will lose the spirit of the thing, will put yourself through a lot of trouble, and will have nothing to show for it after all."

The swordsman was then aware that among the rest there was a large demon whose nose was not so very long and whose wings were not so apparent. His robes and headdress were arranged properly, and he sat elevated above the others. This demon said, "What each of you has argued is not without principle. In the past, martial artists were serious, their resolution was absolutely sincere, they worked soundly on technique, and were neither daunted nor lazy. Such men believed what their instructors passed on to them, made great efforts day and night, tested their techniques, spoke with their friends about their doubts, mastered what they studied, and awakened themselves to principles. For this reason, what they acquired penetrated deeply within them. At first their instructors would teach them techniques, but say nothing of the principles that were hidden within them. They only waited for their students to uncover those principles by themselves. This is called 'drawing [the bow], but not releasing [the arrow].' And it's not that they spoke grudgingly. They simply wanted the students to use their minds, and to master what they were studying in the interval.

Disciples would thoroughly exert their minds and make great efforts. If there was something they understood on their own, they would still go and confront the teacher; and he would acknowledge their understanding when their minds were in accord. If the teacher released [the arrow], nothing would be learned. And this was not just in the martial arts. Confucius said, 'I am not going to go on with the fellow who does not respond by lifting up three corners when I have already lifted up one.'[24] This was the teaching method of the men of old. In this way, the students were sure to be serious whether in scholarship or in the martial arts.

"Nowadays, people are shallow and their resolution is not in earnest. They dislike the strenuous and love the easy from the time they are young. When they see something vaguely clever, they want to learn it right away; but if taught in the manner of the old ways, they think it not worth learning. Nowadays, the way is revealed by the instructor, the deepest principles are taught even to beginners, the end result is set right out in front, and the student is led along by the hand.

"Even with methods like these, students become bored and many of them quit. In this way, talking about principles takes the high seat, the men of old are considered inadequate, mastery becomes watered down, and students only make efforts in things that might have them climb to "new heights." This is, again, the spirit of the times.

"Instructing a man is like training a horse. Simply suppress the ch'i that goes in a distorted way, and you aid the horse to improve its correct ch'i on its own. And don't be oppressive."

The demon continued, "When your mind resides in technique, ch'i overflows and will not be integrated. This could be called 'following the branch and neglecting the stem.' But to say that you 'should not train yourself with complete abandon' is also incorrect. Technique is the function of swordsmanship. If you toss that function aside, how will the very essence of principle be manifested?

"You are enlightened to that essence [or true character] by training function. Becoming enlightened to that essence, you will function with complete freedom. Essence and function are of one origin, are not distinct, and have no interval in between them at all. You may suddenly be enlightened to principle, but if your practice of technique is immature, your ch'i will congeal, and form will have no freedom. Technique is given life by principle; what is without form is the basis of what has form.[25] Thus, it is the order of things that technique is trained by means of ch'i, and that ch'i is trained by means of the mind. Nevertheless, when your practice of technique is mature, you control your ch'i and settle your spirit.

"A boatman grasps the pole and runs along the gunwale, and to him it is just like running along a broad road. How has he become so resourceful? Moreover, when his practice is mature concerning being in the water, he will know how not to perish even if he is drawn into a flood. This is because his spirit is settled and he has complete freedom. The woodcutter shoulders his heavy load of

"A boatman grasps the pole and runs along the gunwale, and to him it is just like running along a broad road. How has he become so resourceful?"

kindling and walks along a narrow trail; the tile master climbs up to the top of a tower and lays out his tiles—in all these cases the practice of technique is mature, there are no doubts and no fears. Thus, the spirit is settled and there is complete freedom.

"Swordsmanship is exactly like this. So when your practice of this art is mature, when it has deeply penetrated your mind, when you have tried your hand at your techniques and there are neither doubts nor fears, your ch'i will be vital, your spirit will be settled, and your practical application will go through its changes with complete freedom and without obstacle.

"Getting to this point, however, is a matter of training your ch'i and coming to know these things on your own. This is what you can rely on. Thus, you may discuss the matter by means of words, but the man who responds naturally—the man who comes without form and goes without a trace,[26] and who has that un-expected mysterious function—has the state of No-Mind. So though you may think that the essence of mind might be passed on consciously, there is actually nothing to receive: you may ask, but there is no one who ought to know, and the instructor has nothing to pass on to you. You can only make great efforts in self-discipline and obtain it naturally. The instructor just points out the path. He cannot talk about it easily. Thus, it is rare in this world."

One of the other demons asked, "If that is so, what about some-one like me who has disciplined himself, but has been unable to attain the Way?"

"...in all these cases, the practice of technique is mature, there are no doubts and no fears. Thus, the spirit is settled and there is complete freedom."

The demon responded, "What do you mean, you can't attain it? You could reach The Goal just by studying the sages. How much more so with a trivial art like swordsmanship. Listen, swordsmanship is the discipline and training of the Great Vitality.[27] So you begin this study by training the ch'i by means of technique. After your beginning studies, you still discipline your ch'i, but move away from technique; yet there should be no point where you try your hand vacantly. You should become mature in your discipline of ch'i, and master the mind. The rate at which you progress during this time will depend on the relative sharpness of your character. It is easy to know the mysterious function of the mind, but difficult to penetrate deep within yourself and act with complete freedom during change.

"Swordsmanship is the art used at the border between life and death. It is easy to throw away your life and proceed toward death, but it is difficult not to make life and death two. The man who does not make life and death two should be easily able to act with complete freedom."[28]

One of the group asked, "Should the Zen monks who have transcended the matter of life and death have perfect freedom in swordsmanship?"

The demon replied, "The aim of their studies is different. Zen monks are weary of the cycle of rebirth and hope to enter Nirvana. They plunge their minds into the jaws of death from the very beginning and extricate themselves from life and death. Even if they were to find themselves in the midst of a great force of the enemy and their bodies were pounded into dust, their minds would not likely be moved at all. But this is not a matter of being able to use one's life; it is simply despising death. This is different from the sages saying that life and death are penetrated with one essence. Entrust life to life, and entrust death to death; but do not make this mind two. Just follow along to the place where significance resides and exert all your energy in that Way. With this, you will gain complete freedom."

Another of the demons asked, "When mind does not enter life and death, they are one. But that is of no use to life. How can this give rise to complete freedom?"

The demon said, "The use of the mind is different from the very beginning. With Nirvana as the main concern, the mind is not used for life. It is only for making a good death. For this reason, it cannot give rise to complete freedom in the function of life.

"The study of the sages does not make life and death two. When confronting life, you put all your power into the Way of life; when confronting death, you put all your power into the Way of death. You do not create the least bit of a concept nor move your mind at all. Thus, in life you have complete freedom; and in death you have complete freedom.[29]

"Now to Zen monks, creation is considered illusion and confusion; and the world of men, a dream and transience. So it is thought that this putting all of one's power into the Way of life is creating an attachment to that life. This can be seen from their ordinary activities. They distance themselves from literature, abandon their lord and vassals, and do not clarify position and stipend.[30] They do not provide for military preparedness, and consider the sages' views of rites, music, punishments, and laws[31] like a baby's way of seeing the world as a plaything. But how can there be mind in tossing aside the ordinary life and unused weapons? Simply, when they meet with death, they do not begrudge their lives; they think only that the entire world is a transformation of the mind."

One of them then asked, "What about the swordsmen of old who encountered Zen monks and were enlightened to the deepest meaning of their art?"

The demon replied, "It is not that the Zen monks were passing on the deepest meaning of swordsmanship. It is simply that when your mind is at peace, you can respond to things easily. You actually harass life when you are attached to it.[32] When your mind is filled with absurd ideas as though the Three Worlds of past, present, and future were enclosed in a cave, it only indicates that your life is in danger.

"The swordsmen you speak of had been resolved toward the martial arts for years. They had not spent easy nights of deep sleep, they had disciplined their ch'i, had done their very best with techniques, and had participated in many matches. Nevertheless, their minds had not been opened. They encountered their Zen priests after passing many years in deep chagrin, and had grasped the principle of life and death on their own. Upon hearing that all phenomena are but a reflection of the mind, their minds were suddenly opened and their spirits settled; they let go of what they had depended on and gained total freedom of action.

"For such men, after many years of training their ch'i and testing their techniques, the vessel became complete. And this is not something that happens abruptly. It is the same as having an awakening under the stick used by Zen patriarchs to arouse sleepy meditators: it is not something that comes all of a sudden. Thus, the person whose art is not yet mature may meet with famous monks of great wisdom, yet he will still not have an awakening."

CHAPTER 2

In all the arts, from *hoka*[33] to Tea Ceremony, one becomes skillful by training in technique. What makes each one singular, however, is ch'i. It is nothing other than the metamorphosis of yin and yang that provides for the great sun and moon that give light to the earth, the coming and going of the heat and cold, and the revolution of the four seasons, and the life and death of all things. Its mysterious function could never be fully explained in words. The Ten Thousand things exist within this, and by means of that ch'i carry out their lives.[34] Ch'i is the very fountain of life. When ch'i departs from form, there is death; and the line between life and death is only the metamorphosis of this ch'i. When you know the fountainhead of life, you know the point where death ends. When the Ways of life and death are clear, that knowledge pervades the hazy and distinct, the demons and gods, and they all become one. For this reason, if you place your body in life at this moment, you will have complete freedom; and if you place your body in death, you will have complete freedom.

In Buddhism there is a pervasive dread of rebirth and transmigration. Thus the Buddhists consider creation and transformation as illusion and confusion, and cut off thought to eliminate discriminating knowledge. Returning to an Emptiness where there is no coming and going, they become Buddhas.

In the Learning of the Sages, however, there is no fear of rebirth and transmigration. They just ride along with change and return as it exhausts itself. Training their ch'i, they come to understand the mind of themselves.

Although the principle of life and death is easy to know, we are reluctant to leave our lives after so short a time. This is called the mind of confusion. Because this mind of confusion acts without reason, our spirits are tormented and we do not realize how we are always suffering defeat.

One of the demons in the group asked, "Although I hesitate to ask to be informed of its most fundamental principles, I would like to hear the gist of ascetic training and discipline."

The demon said, "The Way cannot be seen or heard. What can be seen or heard are just the traces of the Way. But you will be enlightened about what has no traces by the traces themselves. This is called 'receiving it on your own.' If Learning is not receiving it on your own, it will have no function. Though swordsmanship is just a trivial art, it uses the essence of mind and, extended to its most fundamental principle, merges with the Way. Though I myself have not received it on my own, there is something I have heard in secret, and I'll tell you a little bit about that. But listen without discrimination! Don't just listen with your ears![35]

"Look, ch'i controls form by riding the mind. In this way, the function of the body is entirely grasped by ch'i. Now ch'i's spirit is called the mind, and when the mind is equipped with the principle of Heaven, it makes ch'i its foundation. The essence of the mind originally has no shape, sound, color, or smell; but when it rides ch'i, it performs these functions. Ch'i pervades above and below. If you have but the smallest thought, it is possessed by ch'i. It moves when in contact with things in the mind. This is called emotion. When thinking, it goes back and forth, conceptualizing. But when the mind and perceptions move just as they are and your true character is in accord with the principle of Heaven, the spirit is pierced through from beginning to end. The ch'i does not move without reason.

"This is like a boat following a current downstream. Though you can say that it moves, the boat is at rest and there is no trace of that movement. This is called 'moving without moving.'[36]

"The common man has not yet cut though the root of confusion of life and death. This always lies concealed and acts as a cover over the spirit. Thus, before the feelings of joy and anger have arisen, in his dull state of mind it is just like being filled with muddy water. When a thought stirs even a little, what has been concealed arises; his emotions, desires, and irrationalities move, and he is persecuted by his conscience. This is like poling a boat upstream in a flood. Waves rock the boat wildly, and there is no peace within. When ch'i moves randomly, there will be no freedom in practical application.

"Swordsmanship is the technique of contention, and it is considered essential to cut through the root of confusion of life and death from the very beginning of your study. But it is difficult to do this abruptly. For this reason, you should use all the power of your mind to cut through the principle of life and death, to develop your ch'i, to test the techniques of physical confrontation, and make great efforts without any neglect throughout this time. When you have sacrificed your life for training, when your techniques are mature, when your ch'i is under control, when principle has penetrated your mind and you have no doubts, when you are no longer confused and your spirit meets no obstruction—then your thoughts will not move within you at all. And when your thoughts do not move, ch'i will follow spirit. It will move along with animation and will flow smoothly. When ch'i rides the mind, it will not stagnate, it will not be stopped, and it will control form with complete freedom and without obstruction.

"Following the perceptions of the mind, the speed of practical application is like opening a door and the moonlight immediately shining in; or like striking something and having the immediate response of a sound. Victory and defeat are the traces of practical application. But if you don't have conceptualization, form will not have aspect. Aspect is the shadow of concept, and is what manifests form. If there is no aspect to form, the opponent you are supposed to face will not exist. This is what is meant when we say that neither my opponent nor I exist.[37] If I exist, my opponent exists. Because I do not exist, even the insignificant thought of good or evil, perversion or properness, by the man coming at me will be reflected as in a mirror. And this is not reflected from me. It is simply that he arrives and moves on. This is just like being unable to confront with your own wickedness someone who has attained virtue. It is a mystery of the Of-Itself-So. If I tried to divert it from myself, it would become a thought. And because this thought would obstruct me, my ch'i would stagnate, and practical application would not be completely free.[38]

"The person who comes and goes like a god neither thinking about nor enacting the unfettered mysterious function—this is the swordsman who can be said to have attained enlightenment."

The demon continued, "Nevertheless, we demons have long noses, beaks, and wings, and for this reason have spiritual obstructions in other matters. The fact that we are unable to have perfect freedom in practical application of the mind is why we so intently set our sights on this one path from the very beginning, disciplining our minds and cultivating our ch'i. As for those other matters, we forget about those that could help us from distress, and even if they cross in front of us, we don't see them even if our eyes are open. How much more difficult it is for us to restrain our minds!

"Thus, though we train ourselves and grasp this one art clearly, we are unable to understand it in broad terms and apply it elsewhere. There is a limit to the extent of our clarity. For example, it is as though you put a lamp in a box and open just one side. Although the light will shine in that one opened direction, it will not extend elsewhere. That which shines a short distance away will be just a trace of light off to the side. Thus, we are unable to bring ourselves to perfection.

"In the beginning you detect just a small hole, and by using your strength you dig that hole open. By the power of your training, that hole gradually becomes larger and a great deal of light shines through. Then, if you train yourself by using everything in Heaven and Earth as you might a sword, you split that box open and every single direction will be bright.

"When the essence of mind has complete freedom and no obstructions, though our great enemies—wealth and position, poverty and low rank, tribulations and privations—surround us front and back, left and right, our thoughts should not move even a hair's breadth, and it should be like brushing away flies with a round fan. They should all bow down before us, not even daring to lift their heads.

"If we demons could attain this, even our noses would become normal and we would be free to fly without wings."

The demon further spoke, "Generally speaking, the person who has gained proficiency in an art is constantly employing his mind. Thus, he should be quite clear on the principles of that art. But if his determination is aimed at his own art alone, he becomes a specialist and it will be difficult for him to enter the Way. At times there may be someone who is said to be fond of scholastics, but his interests are more truly in the martial arts. The Way then takes second place. Even if such a man hears about deep principles, he takes them all as pertaining to his art and is unable to apply them broadly. So how will this help him in the art of the mind? If the man who is disciplining himself in an art grasps this fact himself, the art that he practices daily will assist his mind, and his mind's fundamental mysterious function will become manifest. In this way, his art too will gain freedom of action.

"Still, there are people who have difficulty in ridding themselves of the concepts to which they have been attached from the very beginning. If they could only let loose of their egotistical interests—whether they be in scholastics or the martial arts—there would be no one under Heaven who could move them, and their practical application would be unhindered and free.

"'Egotistical interests' are not restricted to money, possessions, sensual affairs, or deceptive engagements and the like. If there is the least bit of attachment to any concept, even if it is not a bad one, it is an 'egotistical attachment.' A little attachment clogs up the mind a little, and a great deal of attachment does a great deal of clogging. Now a person who is proficient in an art clearly knows that egotistical interest in techniques will bring him harm. Nevertheless, he may not understand this enough to test it out broadly in terms of practical application of his mind. And though a man may discipline himself in techniques of the mind, if he has learned its principles too quickly and easily, it will be difficult for him to discipline himself in their subtle and hidden concepts.

"The man who cultivates techniques of the mind is yourself; the man who studies the martial arts is also yourself. There are not two minds here. You should reflect on this deeply."

The demon went on, "Nowadays there are many swordsmen whose techniques are mature, whose ch'i is integrated, who have tested their efficiency in combat, who have no doubts, whose spirits are settled, and who have gained freedom in action. Though we may say that they are like gods of that mysterious function, if they have not been able to escape relying on something, they are still like the boatman who runs along the gunwale, or the tile master who climbs up the tower and lays his tiles.[39] These men we call proficient in the martial arts."

One of the group asked, "What about assisting the study of the Way by means of the martial arts now?"

The demon answered, "The mind is nothing but one's nature and emotions. One's nature is the natural law of the essence of the mind. When it is calm and unmoving, it has neither color nor form. But depending on the movement of the emotions, there is wrong, there is right, there is good and there is evil. Look at the mysterious function of the essence of the mind and, according to changes of the emotions, you will understand the difference between natural law and human desires. This is called the art of Learning.[40]

"And what does it mean to know that difference? It is to know that you are already equipped with the spiritual knowledge of your own self-nature, which is divine and neither deceives nor lies. It is not the shallow knowledge and clever wit of people in general. Such knowledge and wit are born from consciousness. Conscious thought is the knowledge of the mind. Although consciousness is based on spiritual clarity, it arises when it is in contact with the good and evil of the emotions. Thus there are thoughts of right, wrong, good, and evil in the consciousness as well. As this consciousness arises, it supports both good and bad emotions, and one's own private cleverness is produced. This is called superficial knowledge.

"Knowledge of your self-nature and spiritual clarity has nothing to do with the good and evil of emotions. It is pure, and where its principle shines there is no self. Thus, neither good nor evil exist there; it is only clarity.

"When consciousness complies with this and does not use personal effort, it is able to restrain the emotions, has no attachments or hindrances, and is permitted to follow the natural law of the essence of the mind. When there are no attachments—either good or evil—or hindrances as the emotions comply with the essence of mind, consciousness and spiritual clarity are in harmony, and the true use of knowledge arises. And when you reach this point, there are no traces left in the wake of consciousness at all. This is called the very mother of conscious thought.

"The emotions support desire, and thus ingenuity and fabrication are born. When these invariably go through a number of different changes, they fetter the essence of mind, and spiritual clarity will be obstructed. This is called the confused mind. Because the common man makes his emotions and desires the mainstays of his mind, he is driven by this confused mind and is unaware of what troubles his spirit.

"Learning sweeps away the doubts of this confused mind, acknowledges the natural principles of the essence of the mind, opens up its spiritual clarity, and follows its natural laws. Learning does not use the artificiality of superficial knowledge. It entrusts things to themselves and is not enlisted into the service of things. It leaves matters to come as they may, and does not seek them out or avoid them.[41]

"Thus, though your thoughts may go on throughout the entire day, your mind will not be troubled because there is no selfishness involved; and though you may labor in affairs throughout the entire day, your spirit will not be perplexed. You entrust yourself to fate, set yourself on righteousness, and have no doubts or delusions. You establish the sincerity of your own mind, your resolve does not bend by even a hair's breadth, and, because you avoid interfering, you do not employ ingenuity or fabrication. You do not hope for advantage and create superficial knowledge for yourself. Entrusting life to life, you put all of your strength into that Way; entrusting death to death, you are comfortable in that return. Though Heaven and Earth go through their changes, your mind is not distracted; though the Ten Thousand Things are concealed and obscured, your mind is not disturbed; and though you think, you are not attached to those thoughts. You act, but rely on nothing. You understand your mind, cultivate your ch'i, and, firm and resolute, are neither daunted nor neglectful. Relaxed and detached, you live neither contending nor oppressing.[42] From the very beginning of your studies, you establish your resolve and consider even the everyday things you hear and see as vessels for training your mind.

"There is neither greater nor lesser in principle, and the deepest laws of swordsmanship do not surpass this fact. Thus in this art, examine yourself through what you have achieved with self-discipline, and verify your mind-technique with your normal everyday activities. If you do this, the art itself should penetrate deep within you and become invaluable in mutual aid and cultivation.[43]

"From the shallows, you enter the depths; stepping up from the base, you climb to the heights. This is how the study of the Way was aided by the martial arts in the past—a method by which in disciplining yourself in one thing, you gained another.

"Probably, by the time a man reaches the age of fifty, his hands and feet no longer work freely; or, if he is ill or has some sort of employment, he will have no leisure. Thus he will be unable to exert himself in techniques. And if he has the profession of a warrior, he will not be happy with himself when he is not using his mind.

"Yet, even if a man's hands and feet are handicapped and his attention is divided, he should be resolved to discipline himself so that his mind will not be divided. As I have said before, if he does this and establishes his resolve, disciplines himself so that his mind does not fluctuate, makes clear the principle that life and death have a single consistency, and lets none of the Ten Thousand Things in Heaven and Earth become obstacles; then, even if he must lie in bed or has to work as a circulating watchman, he will discipline his mind, and use the things he sees and hears that move through his mind as he would use a sword.

"If you have leisure, you meet with a man accomplished in the martial arts, study his technique, become informed of its principles, and verify them in your mind. When you meet an opponent, you simply execute the action appropriate to you, and happily look death in the face. What then could distress you? It is considered essential not to break the sole resolve of a proper cultured warrior.

"In form there is age and youth, strength and weakness, and deterioration and health. There is also work. All of these are created by Heaven, received by us, but are not of our own doing. When you have that sole resolve, neither Heaven and Earth nor the gods and demons can take it away from you.[44]

"For this reason, entrust the creation of form to Heaven, and simply take care of your own resolve. Men of little character begrudge what Heaven has made, and labor over their own creations. But our intelligence does not reach Heaven's doings. The man who is distressed by things that our intelligence does not reach—and so discomforts himself and the gods—is a fool."

One of the other demons asked, "I have a number of children, but they have not yet grown up. How should I have them study swordsmanship?"

The demon answered, "In the old days, mind-technique would become manifest after first 'sprinkling the ground and sweeping up, and answering and replying,'[45] then studying the Six Arts, and finally entering the Great Learning. Among all the gentlemen of the Confucian school, there were many who became adept at the Six Arts and then verified the study of the Way.

"While your children are still young, they will not have the power to master the connection between technique and principle, so do not bring up details first. Rather, have them follow along with their teacher, make efforts in the techniques that are appropriate for the moment, learn the movements of the hands and feet, and strengthen their bones and sinews. Beyond that, they should train their ch'i and cultivate their minds. The deepest principles will be inferred from this training. This is the proper order of training.

"You should not use a tree that has only two leaves as a pillar. Usually, you prop up a brace and support such a tree so that it will not grow crooked. And usually, from the time a person is young, you should not let him go along with a will toward the perverse. If his will does not go toward the perverse, there will be no wrong, even in play. When there is no wrong, there will be no harm done to what is correct. Between Heaven and Earth, it is rare for someone not to be of some use. But when we do harm due to perversity, and so damage our self-nature, we are of no use at all.

"Fundamentally, man's mind is not without good. It is simply that from the moment he has life, he is always being brought up with perversity. Thus, having no idea that he has gotten used to being soaked in it, he harms his self-nature and falls into evil. Human desire is the root of this perversity.

"Men of little character develop their minds in simply benefiting themselves. Thus, if they do benefit themselves and some perversity is the outcome, they are not aware of that perversity; and, if they do not benefit themselves, but there is some propriety as the outcome, they are unaware of that propriety as well. They do not know how to distinguish between perversity and propriety of themselves. How much less will they understand the results of the two?

"Thus, Learning suppresses the confused actions of man's desires, perceives the mysterious function of the natural principles of the essence of the mind, and makes clear the understanding of the results of perversity and propriety. Only in spurning the perversity of the confused mind is no harm done to the essence of mind or to our self-nature. This is not a matter of rising up to Heaven or sinking down to Earth. It is simply that when you spurn perversity, natural principle is manifest. If you suppress perversity just a little, then natural principle is manifest just a little; if you suppress perversity a great deal, natural principle will be manifested a great deal. You should test this out in your own mind.

"Swordsmanship is just like this. If from the time the student is a beginner without having learned any techniques well, you say something like, 'Technique will come naturally without intention; establish the hard by means of the soft,' or 'Techniques are only trivialities,' he will become empty-headed and lazy, and will know nothing of where to stand. Thus he will be at a loss both in this world and the next."

CHAPTER 3

One of the demons asked, "What is it to move without moving, and to be at rest without being at rest?"

The demon said, "Man is a moving thing. He is incapable of not moving. There are many different responses to man's daily needs, but for one who has grasped the Way, his mind is not moved by phenomena. The essence of the mind is selfless and without desire, and thus at peace and undisturbed.

"Speaking in terms of swordsmanship, when a man is surrounded by a large force and is moving this way and that, if he has resolved the matter of life and death, settled his spirit, and does not have his thoughts rattled by that large force, he will be moving without moving.

"Haven't you seen a man riding on a horse? The man who rides well runs the horse to the east and west, but his mind is tranquil and his unhurried body is unmoving and at peace. Seen from the side, the horse and the man seem to be firmly fastened together. And if he simply restrains the horse's errors, he will be doing nothing contrary to the horse's nature. Thus, though the man is mounted on the saddle and is master of the horse, the horse is not troubled by this and moves with its own understanding. The

"Haven't you seen a man riding on a horse? The man who rides well runs the horse to the east and west, but his mind is tranquil and his unhurried body is unmoving and at peace."

horse forgets the man, the man forgets the horse, and their spirits are one and do not go in different ways. You could say that there is no man in the saddle, and no horse under it.

"This is a manifested form of moving without moving that is easy to see.

"An unskillful rider will go against the horse's nature, and will himself be ill at ease. When the horse and rider are always separate and at odds, the whole frame of the rider's body will move, his mind will be preoccupied with the horse's gait, and the horse too will be tired and troubled.

"In a certain riding manual there is a poem [supposedly] written by a horse:

> He whips me,
>   As if to go,
> Then pulls on the reins;
>   My mouth drawn down,
>   I can't even move.

"This is something that informs us of the horse's emotions instead of our own. And this is not just for horses. You should have this mentality for working with people as well. When you run contrary to the heart of everything and apply learned details first, you yourself will be preoccupied and others will be vexed.

"And what is it to be at rest though not at rest? Before joy and anger, grief and pleasure issue forth, the essence of the mind is transparent and contains absolutely nothing. In the midst of this ultimate peace and absence of desire, when external phenomena arrive, the mind responds, but is not attached to its functions. It is the essence of the mind that is at peace and does not move. What moves and responds to things is the function of the mind. The essence is at peace and contains the myriad of principles and the clarity of spiritual strength. Function follows the laws of the universe and responds to innumerable situations. Essence and function are of one origin. This is what is called moving but not moving, and being at rest but not being at rest.

"To speak of this in terms of swordsmanship, let us say that you take up a weapon and face your opponent. Your opponent comes at you while you are completely at peace, without malice and without fear. Moving this way and that without any thought or concept, you are able to respond freely without any obstructions. Though your body moves, you do not lose the peaceful essence of your mind; though you are at rest, you do not lack the function of movement. A mirror itself is at rest and contains nothing. It allows ten thousand shapes to come and be reflected, and manifests their forms. Yet when they move on, no shadow or shape remains.[46] The metaphor of the moon in the water is the same. And the clear spiritual strength of the essence of the mind is also like this.

"When men of little character move, they are drawn by that movement and lose themselves. When they are at rest, they become empty-headed and are unable to respond functionally."

One of the group asked, "What does 'the moon in the water' mean?"

The demon said, "There are various meanings attached to this phrase according to different schools, but fundamentally 'the moon reflected in the water' is a metaphor for when you can move and respond with spontaneity and No Mind. Among the poems of the Abdicated Emperor Sutoku[47] while he was at the palace near Hirozawa Pond is the following:

> Though there is a reflection,
>> The moon reflects itself
> Without thought.
>> Without thought, too, the water:
>> Hirozawa Pond.

"At the heart of this poem is an enlightened state of mind concerning action and response with No Mind and spontaneity. This is, moreover, like the single full moon shining in the sky while all of the ten thousand rivers and streams contain their own one moon. This is not a matter of the light being divided and then striking the water. If there were no water, there would be no reflection. Again, this is not a matter of the moon being reflected as soon as it is received by the water.[48] Whether it is reflected into ten thousand streams or does not go beyond a single puddle, the moon is neither added to nor subtracted from. And again, it does not select either a large or small body of water.

"From this you should be awakened to the mysterious function of the essence of the mind.

"The last thing to be spoken of here would be the water's clarity or muddiness. Nevertheless, while the moon has a shape and a color, there is neither shape nor color to the mind. This is just a metaphor for something easily seen with shape and color, and something that has neither. All of these metaphors are just like this. You should not become attached to the metaphor and thus chisel away at the mind."

Another in the group asked, "All the schools of swordsmanship speak of the 'remaining mind.'[49] I wonder, what does this term mean?"

The demon replied, "This refers only to the point where the essence of the mind is not affected by one's technique and does not move. When the essence of the mind does not move, action and response are clear. Everyday human affairs are just like this.

"Even if I were to leap up and plunge right to the bottom of Hell, I would still be the same fundamental I. Thus, I am unobstructed and free both in front and behind and to the left and right. This is not a matter of inserting the mind and keeping it there. When the mind remains, it is divided into two. Moreover, when the essence of the mind is not clear and the mind is consciously inserted, there will only be blind striking and blind thrusting. Clarity is born from the unmoving essence of the mind, and then there is simply striking with clarity and thrusting with clarity. This is difficult to discuss. If you understand it poorly, it will result in great harm."

The demon continued, "In all the schools of swordsmanship there is something called 'initiative.'[50] This is also used for the sake of the beginner to express how to aid his ardor and how to spur him on against indolence. In fact, when the essence of the mind does not move and you do not lose yourself, and when expansive ch'i fills the body, you will always have initiative.

"This is not a matter of striking a person first or of using the mind. Fundamentally, it is considered essential in swordsmanship to nourish your basic vitality and to avoid a spirit of death. To attack in the midst of waiting, or to wait in the midst of attacking are both spontaneous action and response. Initiative is really just a provisional name used for the sake of beginners, but at its heart it means moving while not moving, and being at rest while not being at rest.

"If a beginner cannot speak about the application of techniques based on hard and soft ch'i, he will have nothing to rely on. Thus, you give names to such things and teach in that way. When you give something a name, however, you may become attached to that name and misunderstand the fundamental principle. But if you don't give things names and leave them blank, the student may not comprehend the full meaning.

"At any rate, there is no way you can talk about it with a person who has not grasped an understanding of the general meaning. And all techniques are like this. So if the person who would teach something does not have a suitable student, it would be better for him to keep quiet and not talk at all without circumspection. If a student has grasped the gist of the subject, he will quickly understand from what he has seen and heard."

The demon went on, "As I explained before, activity or rest throughout the body is entirely a function of ch'i. Thus, the mind is the soul[51] of ch'i, and ch'i is simply yin and yang, pure or muddy. When ch'i is pure, there is activity and lightness of function; when it is muddy, there is stagnation and heaviness of function. Form follows ch'i, and for this reason in swordsmanship it is considered essential to train your ch'i. When ch'i is active, practical application is light and swift; when it is muddy, practical application is heavy and slow.

"Although a vigorous ch'i is respected, when your vigor is used with partiality and harmony is neglected, it becomes fragmented and its function cannot be put into practice. A person who relies on such will leave nothing behind but empty actions without use. And though, when it comes to function we respect harmony, when vigor is not the master within it, it flows away and results in weakness. Now the weak and the soft are different altogether. The soft contains living ch'i and performs function. The weak is simply not strong, and is unable to perform function. Being at rest and being inert are also completely different. Being at rest does not distance itself from living ch'i, but being inert is slightly removed from it.

"A person who is tense relies on ch'i but has difficulty in loosening it. Relying on thoughts or concepts, you will become taut. The ch'i of yin becomes taut on its own, and the person who relies altogether on ch'i will not be swift in responding to some action. Thus, a tense or taut ch'i will be slow in its function of technique. But the person whose ch'i goes first will dry up his technique's practical application. This is yang, and lacks foundation. It will be light and parched, and will be like withered leaves scattered by the wind.

"The person who is too damp and stagnant will be dragged down by a muddy ch'i that is heavy of itself and will be slow in practical application. The person who is too concentrated will focus on ch'i with partiality, and will render his form shackled and rigid. He will come to a standstill and will be unable to move. Thus his action and response will be all the slower, like a stream that has frozen and is unable to melt. This, again, is the congealing of thought and the congealing of ch'i. What we call thought is also ch'i. The known is called thought; the unknown is called ch'i. You should test this out and know it on your own."[52]

The demon continued, "The man who has complete freedom in changing between the hard and the soft will have no obstructions in his actions and responses. And this is not just in swordsmanship alone. Even in Learning, if a man studies and grasps this complete freedom in changing between the hard and the soft in ch'i, he will be able to manifest the mysterious function of the mind.

"The mysterious function of the essence of the mind leaves no traces and cannot be explained. Thus, in swordsmanship you develop yourself by means of ch'i, and know how to manifest the essence of the mind. In Learning you develop yourself by means of the mind and know the mysterious function of the metamorphosis of ch'i. Nevertheless, when you only know this in terms of principle within your consciousness and do not cultivate it and grasp it with your body, the mind knows ch'i only by hearsay and will be unable to perform its function. A swordsman may cultivate his ch'i, but if he only develops it in terms of the practical application of swordsmanship, the spirit of Learning in his mind will be only one-directional, and that cultivation will not extend to his daily activities.

"The mind is fundamentally one with ch'i. If you test this out for yourself and grasp the gist of it, you should be able to perform appropriately with improvement even though your training is not yet mature."

The demon spoke further, "For all the schools of swordsmanship, when it comes to the deepest principle, there is only one. It is simply that each of the various styles leads out from the door thought to be good by the founder who trained and cultivated himself, putting his entire being into it. But there are many who love the landscape along the way, and who live in that landscape, thinking it to be the Truth. Because of this, you see the many branching styles fighting among themselves over what is right and wrong. But the fundamental principle is not something that can be fought about in terms of what is right and wrong. The landscape along the way is nothing more than what is in your own consciousness; there are not two or three Great Fundamentals.

"When you make divisions, there is good and evil, perversion and propriety, hard and soft, and long and short. But you will never cease to argue on the ramifications of branches and shoots. It is foolish to think that another person doesn't know what you know. If you have spiritual clarity, another person will have spiritual clarity as well. How could you be the only knowledgeable one while everyone else under heaven is a fool?

"Thus, there is nothing that is hidden. And it is just like this in Learning. For the disciples of Lao Tzu, the Buddha, Chuang Tzu, Lieh Tzu, Ch'ao Fu, and Hsu Yu,[53] they were one in seeing the essence of mind in selflessness and absence of desire. Thus, they had not a hair's breadth of selfish thought in their heads to encumber them. It was simply that the landscape they saw was different, and so in their separation, their schools were different.

"The Way of the sages crowns itself with Heaven and places its feet upon the earth, and so does not leave the mountains and rivers or the solid ground behind. It takes interest in knowing the foolishness or incompetence of the common husband and wife, and will enact them out as well.

"There is no one under heaven not gifted with humanity and righteousness, and no one to vilify for their lack of filial piety, obedience to elders, loyalty, or good faith. Even the disciples of the Buddha from India receive the blessings of the sages and are bathed in their humanity and righteousness.

"This is not in a place that can be reached by the landscapes of the different schools. And that is because you see it by looking down from the Great Foundation of Heaven and Earth and the Ten Thousand Things. The disciples of the different schools are all just different factions of the sages. They are unable to turn their backs on the Great Way."

One of the group asked, "Purity and muddiness are yin and yang. Why should we only employ purity and avoid muddiness?"

The demon replied, "There are points when you will use muddiness as well, although in swordsmanship celerity is favored. You cannot do without yin and yang. It is simply that you use clarity and avoid the weight of muddiness. In drying things you use fire, you do not use water. It is just that each has its own use. The mind's clarity or dullness is again nothing more than the clarity or muddiness of ch'i. Clarity of ch'i shelters the spiritual awakening of self-nature. Matter is of itself intelligent. The essence of the mind is fundamentally mysterious and omniscient. It is simply that when muddy ch'i covers the mind's spiritual clarity, foolishness, stupidity, and dull-wittedness are born. Something that is confused or contrary to reason we call foolishness. The stagnant and slow we call dull-witted. Muddy ch'i is extraordinarily heavy, we are pulled back by its sediment, our thoughts become entrenched, and we are confused and lost in darkness. We are unable to set aside our thinking. We are unable to become settled ourselves, nor are we able to follow others. Always perplexed, we are unable to stop. This is called stupidity. While we say that the character of the common man has infinite variety, it is all just a matter of the muddiness of his ch'i: how shallow or deep, how thick or thin.

"The mind is the soul of ch'i. This is not to say that where this ch'i exists there is no soul. If there is no ch'i, there is no soul. Again, this is like a person riding in a boat, crossing over the water. When the wind is violent and the waves rough, the boat follows the wind and is pulled by the waves; no one knows where it's going to go, and the people inside the boat are uneasy. The phenomenon of muddy ch'i moving in confusion and the mind not being at peace is just like this. When the wind stops and the waves die down, they return to their original state, and the people in the boat are able to feel at ease.

"Man creates perversity in his mind and puts his body in danger. This is nothing but the confused action of muddy ch'i. Its foundation is the typhoon that blows out of the cave of desire. Desire itself is an inclination of muddy ch'i. When an eccentric person has strong emotions and passions, the yin ch'i will congeal and strengthen. Someone whose mind is agitated and without self-confidence will lack the foundation of yang ch'i. An apprehensive person will starve his ch'i and his body will not be replete. A person unable to fix his mind will have weak ch'i and will be unsettled. He will also be close to stupidity. These are all maladies of muddy ch'i.

"Now, a person who is deliberate and quick of mind will integrate yin and yang, and will lack nothing. A man whose intelligence is discerning but whose activities are not deliberate, will have a dominant, clear yang ch'i, but the vitality of his yin will be weak. The man whose activity is deliberate but who lacks discerning intelligence will have a dominant yin vitality, but his clear yang ch'i will be weak.

"For that contained by the yang within the yin, or the yin within the yang—one could never come to an end of discussing excess or deficiency, the shallow and the deep, the thick and the thin, or all the other innumerable variables. When you conjecture about the varieties or imagine the details, none are excluded from yin and yang, clarity and muddiness. From the vastness of Heaven and Earth at the top to tiny beings like lice and fleas below, if they are not replete with the ch'i of yin and yang, they will be unable to perform the functions of their forms.

"At this time I've discussed only the gist of this matter"

Another in the group asked, "How do I cultivate this ch'i?"

The demon answered, "It is only in avoiding its muddiness. The ch'i of yin and yang is active and, going through changes and metamorphoses, is the Great Fundamental of Heaven, Earth, and the Ten Thousand Things. Muddiness is the sediment and dregs of yin and yang. Dregs and sediment have come to a halt and are not active. Moving with the aid of yang, their function is heavy and slow. This is like when you add mud to clear water and immediately have muddy water. When you have muddy water, you can't cleanse things. If you sprinkle things with it, you just make them dirty. Thus, the art of Learning does nothing more than use the clarity of intuition to clear away muddiness. When you have cleared away muddiness, your ch'i will be lively, the essence of mind will manifest itself alone, and the confused mind will turn immediately into the Original Mind.

"The mind, after all, is not two."

The demon continued, "Although yin and yang are fundamentally of one ch'i, as soon as you divide them, innumerable differences arise. When you obscure the differences of their functions without knowing that they are originally one, the Way will be unclear. When you know that they are originally one but are not aware of their different functions, you will be unable to put the Way into action. Simply test this out in your mind, and make efforts in its details. Explaining it in words would never come to an end. It is only because you demons up here in the leafy trees have not fully understood the essence of the mind that I have expounded now in terms of existence and non-existence.

"This mind exists in the center of ch'i, just as a fish swims in water. A fish has freedom according to the depth of the water. If a large fish is not in a deep pool, it will not be able to swim. And if the water starts to dry up, the fish will be in trouble. When the water is all gone, the fish will die. The mind has freedom according to the vigor of the ch'i. When there is a lack of ch'i, the mind thins out; when ch'i is exhausted, the mind returns to Non-Existence. Thus, when water churns up, the fish are startled; and when ch'i is in motion, the mind will not be calm."

The demon continued, "This is not limited to matters of physical confrontation. In all things it is different to entrust matters to Heaven or to entrust them to fate. In swordsmanship, you always thoroughly investigate the principles of physical confrontation; in human affairs, you stay within the principles of justice natural to those affairs, and employ none of your own personal cleverness. You act, but are not dependent on anything; you think, but are not bound to those thoughts. This is called entrusting things to Heaven. It is like a farmer working in agriculture: he tills the soil, plants the seeds, weeds skillfully, and leaves no stone unturned in the Way at which he should be so proficient. But he entrusts those things beyond his control—such as floods, droughts, and typhoons—to Heaven.

"When you leave things to Heaven, but have not done everything you could in human affairs, you will not have understood Heaven's Way. You will just be waiting for things to happen of their own accord, and this is called entrusting things to fate. For the moment, however, it could be said that if you are confused and unsettled, you should go ahead and leave things to fate."

One of the other demons asked, "The essence of the mind has no form, color, sound, or scent. The Mysterious Function is spirit and its principles cannot be known. How then can we train our minds?"

The demon said, "The essence of the mind cannot be put into words. Simply control the excess or insufficiency of the movement of the seven emotions [pleasure, anger, sorrow, joy, love, hate, and desire] or in the awareness of your own consciousness during the moments of action and response. Avoid the confused action of your own selfish thoughts, and follow the natural principles of your own self-nature. Putting your hand to this will depend on the revelation of your own intuition. What is this 'intuition?' It is a knowledge that illuminates truth and falseness, perversity and propriety with the spiritual clarity of the essence of the mind, and is conversant with the very essence of Heaven and Earth.

"For the common man, this knowledge is clouded over by the confused action of muddy ch'i, and is unable to illuminate these things completely. But that which even barely perceives these things as through the slightest fissure is called 'intuition.' With a single thought, you know what is true and what is not, you perceive a man's sincerity, and know when you yourself have done something wrong and are unhappy in your heart of hearts.

"The moving emotions create a mind that is apprehensive about the welfare of others, sympathetic, and full of pity. It is inevitable that we love out parents, are affectionate to our children, and associate properly with the members of our family. This is 'intuition.' When you believe in this intuition and follow it, when you foster it and do no harm because of your own selfish thoughts, the confused actions of muddy ch'i will quiet down on their own. The spiritual clarity of natural principle will manifest itself and itself alone.

"Selfish thoughts are born from a mind bent on its own profit. And when you think only about your own profit, you will not think twice about how you harm others. In the end, you will create perversity, generate evil, and even destroy your own body.

"Cultivating your mind and cultivating ch'i are not two different things. Thus, Mencius lectured on nurturing a vigorous ch'i. And this is simply in having the will to do so; it is not necessarily in making great efforts to foster that ch'i."

Another of the group asked, "In Buddhism, consciousness is detested and avoided. What is this all about?"

The demon answered, "I don't know anything about the ideas of the Buddhists, but consciousness is fundamentally a function of knowledge, and is nothing to abhor. You only dislike it when it aids the passions, distances itself from the essence of the mind, and takes over entirely.

"Consciousness is like a rank-and-file soldier. If the rank and file are kept in the dark by a general, they will become bewildered and lose their vigor. When this occurs, they will not obey the commander's orders, they will put themselves first, use their own contrivances, act selfishly, and disrupt the harmony of the camp. Acting in confusion, they will cause an uproar and finally bring on the calamity of defeat. When it gets to this point there is nothing the general can do. It has been said since times past that when a large army is in turmoil, there is nothing that can be done to calm it down.

"When consciousness takes over entirely, it aids the passions and acts in confusion. And although it may know that it is doing wrong even at the time, it will be difficult to regulate itself. But this is not a matter of consciousness being evil. When the general has wisdom and valor and his orders are clear, the rank and file will be respectful of those orders and not act on their own. Following those orders, they will be able to defeat the enemy; and having made their preparations firm, they will be undefeatable. In this case, the general will be able to accomplish meritorious deeds because of the actions of his rank and file.

"Thus, the consciousness follows the spiritual clarity of the essence of the mind, depends on the natural laws of its self-nature, and performs knowledgeably. If it does not take over entirely and act on its own, it will activate knowledge, and aid in the administration of the state.

"Why then should we abhor consciousness? When the sages said, 'Be warned against consciousness,' they meant that consciousness should not take over entirely, that all wisdom follows the laws of our self-nature, and that consciousness should leave no traces. This is being warned against consciousness."

Another demon asked, "Have there not been traditions of swordsmanship even in China since long ago?"

The demon answered, "I have not yet seen any of their documents. But in the past, in both China and Japan, they put emphasis on the strength and vitality of ch'i, and didn't think twice about life and death. And it appears that they fought with energy. When you look at Chuang Tzu's chapter, *A Discussion on Swords*,[54] it is all like this. And in the chapter, *Mastering Life*,[55] there is a talk on raising fighting cocks. This is entirely concerned with the deepest principles of swordsmanship, but Chuang Tzu was not discussing it for the sake of that art. He was only discussing the maturity arrived at by the cultivation of ch'i.

"There are not two principles here. The words of enlightened men communicate all principles secretly. If you use your mind, all things will have to do with either Learning *or* swordsmanship. When you look at the documents on swordsmanship in Japan from long ago, there were never any elevated theories. You only see lessons on the achievement of lightness and speed. And many of the styles consider demons as their predecessors. When you think about it, they were all endowed with an inherent courage, but there is no talk about this at all. It is apparent that they simply learned their profession, trained their ch'i, and in doing so, cultivated their inherent courage. Thus, there was no reason to talk about it.

"Nowadays, the world has become quite civilized, and though abstruse principles are discussed from the very beginning of a student's studies, it is like something left on deposit, and its reality is far from having reached that of the ancients. Learning, too, is like this."

Yet another in the group asked, "Swordsmanship is the mysterious function of the mind. Why then are there secret techniques?"

The demon said, "The principles of swordsmanship are the

principles of Heaven and Earth. How could there be no one else in the world who knows what I know? Secret things are for the sake of beginners. If they were not kept secret, beginners would not believe in them. This is one of the expedients of teaching. Thus, the things that are kept secret are just the tail-ends of techniques. They are not in some deep principle. Beginners understand nothing, listen arbitrarily, grasp things poorly, and decide 'This is it!' on their own. So contrary to what you might expect, they cause damage when they speak with others.

"For this reason you can see that you should not teach except to those who will grasp the meaning of what you say. But though you talk about the 'deepest principles' even to people outside of your own school, you may speak openly and still have nothing to hide.

"Hidden things are for the most part expedients in teaching the martial arts. Keeping things secret from a student who is not yet mature is yet another stratagem for aiding his ability to some day prevail over others. Moreover, when others see such things, they will not understand their significance. Thus, to keep them hidden is to spare oneself of others denigrating them as shallow or criticizing them as unreasonable.

"As a rule, you should not discuss these things at all. Although all techniques are not hidden in the True Way, words leak out and cause harm. Thus, according to the material, there are some things that should be kept secret and concealed.

"There is no difference in the principle of technique in swordsmanship and the technique of practical application in the world at large. In the technique of swordsmanship you employ the mind and distinguish propriety and perversity, and truth and falsehood, in detail. If you try this in the midst of your everyday affairs and reach the point where perversity is unable to prevail over propriety, this in itself is a great advancement."

The demon went on, "It is considered essential that the mind be made clear and have no obstruction. It is considered essential that the ch'i be made vigorous and unyielding. Mind and ch'i are fundamentally of one essence. If you were to speak of separating them, they would be like fire and firewood. There is no greater or lesser to fire. If the firewood is insufficient, the fire will have no kindling power. When the firewood is damp, the flame will not be bright.

"All of the functions of man's body are operated by ch'i. Thus, a person with a vigorous ch'i will have no illnesses, and will not be sensitive to wind, cold, heat, or dampness. The person whose ch'i is weak will easily become ill, and will be quick to feel pestilential vapors. When the ch'i is infirm, the mind is afflicted and the body is exhausted. In a medical book it states, 'The hundred diseases all spring from ch'i.' The person who does not understand the changes ch'i goes through will not understand how diseases come about. Thus it is considered fundamental that a man cultivate a vigorous and active ch'i.

"There is a Way to cultivate ch'i. If the mind is not full of clarity, ch'i will lose its way and act in confusion. When ch'i acts in confusion, it loses the mainstays of vigor and resolution, and quickly obscures the clear wisdom of the mind with superficial knowledge. When the mind acts foolishly and the ch'i moves in confusion, you may be full of youthful vigor, but your techniques will not have complete freedom. Youthful vigor is only temporary and is not rooted. Moving, its imprints will be empty. You should try out and understand these things with the techniques of swordsmanship.

"Thus, the samurai-scholar who is just beginning his studies first puts all of his effort into the human affairs of filial piety, and avoids human desires. When he does act with desire or confusion, he will restrain his ch'i and not become attached. Acting with vigor and resolution, he will be able to reinforce his clarity of mind. But when his ch'i is not vigorous, his affairs will not be settled; and from this lack of resolution, he will employ superficial knowledge and obstruct the clarity of the essence of mind. This is called delusion.

"Swordsmanship is also just like this. When your spirit is settled and your ch'i integrated, when your action and response comes with No-Mind and techniques follow naturally, you will have reached the deepest principles. Nevertheless, if in the beginning you do not develop a deep and active ch'i, abandon superficial knowledge, and develop an infallible temperament that would spread your opponents at your feet and have you break through an 'iron wall,' then you will be unable to mature and reach the farthest point of departure of No-Mind and the spontaneity. What you think is No-Mind will be obstinate vacuity, and what you think is integration will be indolent ch'i.

"This is not so in swordsmanship alone. In archery, horseman-ship, or any of the martial arts, if you do not first establish an indefatigable will and cultivate a vigorous and active ch'i, it will come to nothing. Ch'i is fundamentally vigorous, and is the ori-gin of life. Man does not simply lack in its cultivation. Because he damages it with superficial knowledge, he becomes cowardly and does not put it to use. And all the affairs of this world are like this.

"As I explained previously, ch'i rides the mind and performs the functions of the entire body. You should test this out and come to understand it personally. If you only read about this in books or hear about it in the words of others, and do not try it out personally, it will only be a rumor of true Reason, and you will not be able to employ it physically. This is called learning by Hearsay. In Learning, in the martial arts and in all things, when you hear about principles, try them out yourself, and prove them to your own mind, you will be someone who knows with cer-tainty the perversity, propriety, difficulty, or easiness of a matter. This is called training."

CHAPTER 4

One of the other demons asked, "In the traditional teachings on the spear, there is the straight spear, the cross-headed spear, the hook-spear, the tube-spear,[56] and others. Which of these would be the most advantageous?"

The demon replied, "How can you ask such a stupid question? The spear is a weapon for thrusting, and complete freedom in thrusting is within yourself, not the instrument. Nevertheless, there are people who use spears with sickles attached, spears with shafts fashioned with hooks, and spears with tubes slipped over the handles. Such people make efforts with the benefits grasped by their predecessors, delve deeply into the operation of these instruments, and use them with freedom. Nowadays, if a person who studies one of these styles practices with his instrument from the beginning, he will be more skillful with that instrument than with others, and will have an abundance of advantages in using it. Becoming accomplished and reaching the point where he has grasped things on his own, even the staff he holds can become a spear for him.

"Thereafter, these schools gather their students together and, after explaining their own special weapon, demonstrate the tubed

"The spear is a weapon for thrusting, and complete freedom in thrusting is within yourself, not the instrument."

or straight spear, or how to defeat an opponent with a hook-shafted spear. This, however, is nothing more than teaching their students how to respond to other weapons, and elucidating the benefits of their own. If they didn't do this, there would be no benefit in carrying the weapon of their own particular style.

"But if you understand this to be the deepest principle here, and think that a sickle-spear is only good for thrusting or that a hooked spear can only entangle itself around the shaft of a straight spear, you will be greatly mistaken. Still, it is vital that the teachings of the schools' founders be mastered wholeheartedly. Understanding them poorly will give rise to the confusion of a beginning student."

The demon continued, "I will now briefly mention the technique of composing the ch'i for those who have not yet been introduced to its initial studies. This is something that even a youngster should emulate.

"First, lie down on your back, relax your shoulders, let your chest and shoulders open up to the right and left, and stretch your arms and legs out comfortably. Place your hands on the empty area in the region of your navel, calmly forget about all your Ten Thousand Thoughts, and empty your mind of all things. Dissolve all obstructions to your ch'i and draw it downward. Let your ch'i fill your entire body, and have it diffuse all the way to the tips of your fingers. Count your incoming and outgoing breaths like the breathing meditation in Buddhism. At first, your breathing will be rough. When it gradually calms down, your ch'i will become lively and should feel as though it fills Heaven and Earth. This is not a matter of holding your breath or straining your ch'i. In this case, your ch'i fills you internally and becomes active.

"At this point, a person suffering an illness will no doubt feel uncomfortable in the location of the disease between his chest and belly. This is the movement of the collected and coagulated ch'i trying to loosen and integrate itself, and there will be a rumbling in the belly. When this happens, many people are surprised by the uncomfortable feeling in their belly and quit altogether. At this time, the ch'i that began to open up and fill the body will be unable to adjust itself, so you should lightly massage the area with the palm of your hand. If it is wrenched too strongly, the poison being moved will reverse itself, and—contrary to what you desire—will not become tranquil. It is different yet when it pushes upward and nauseates you. Generally speaking, when you place your hand in one place over your belly for a while, the ch'i will gather in that place. Thus, this is a practice of not placing your hand over an area that is abundant with ch'i, but rather over a place empty of it.

"Again, a person who has a disease in his back will probably feel uncomfortable there. He should simply perform an action to ensure that his ch'i is not coagulated. The practice is one of opening up the shoulders and the chest. When you open up both shoulders as though they were drawn out, your ch'i will expand. This is a technique of opening up your ch'i with form. When the ch'i is stagnant, the mind is stagnant. When the mind is stale, the ch'i is also stale. The mind and ch'i are of one essence. This technique is one that first opens up the stagnation of ch'i, and then calms the places that are inclined toward that stagnation.

"For example, if your entire body were covered with something like a swarm of ants, you would brush them off and clean yourself up. Then you would put on new clothing and sit down in a clean place. Now, there is something in Shinto called Internal Cleansing and External Cleansing. Internal Cleansing is purifying the mind and avoiding the defilements of selfish thoughts and lascivious ideas. It is returning to the fundamental essence of No-Desire and No-Self, and nourishing your original natural Truth. External Cleansing is making the body clean and renewing your clothing and residence. By altering your ch'i so that external poisons do not become internal, you actually support Internal Cleansing.

"Mind and ch'i are fundamentally of one essence. Ch'i is carried along within form, and performs the function of the mind. Mind is the soul. Having no form, it is the mainstay of ch'i. When you cultivate ch'i, the mind is at peace of itself. When ch'i moves in confusion, the mind is perplexed. For example, it is like when a boat is moving tranquilly, the passengers are at peace; but when the waves are rough and the boat is in danger, the passengers are uneasy. Thus, wherever the student applies his hand, he should first dissolve the coagulation of ch'i and put the mind at peace. He should make his ch'i active and create total freedom for his mind.

"Up to this point I have explained the technique for regulating a scattered ch'i while lying down, and for untwisting a distorted ch'i and putting it at peace. If you practice like this for five, seven, ten, or twenty days, you should have a feeling of being refreshed. When you have this refreshed feeling, you should practice this technique all the more.

"If you are able to regulate your ch'i, it should become active, and you should not be drawn in by an inert ch'i. If you activate your mind even a little as though your entire body were filled with ch'i, your ch'i will become active as well.

"Moreover, when you get up at daybreak, you should assume a correct posture, and enliven your ch'i as though to fill your entire body. You should sit, concentrating inwardly for a while in the *Nio-zazen* style of Shozan,[57] controlling your ch'i. This is not necessarily a matter of lighting an incense stick, fixing a time period, or sitting in the correct Buddhist zazen posture. It is just sitting in your usual fashion, in a proper posture, and enlivening your ch'i. You should train yourself to sit like this for a little while several times a day whenever you have some free time. If you do this, your sinews and bones will be measured and coordinated, your blood will flow without obstruction, your ch'i will have substance, and illnesses will disappear of themselves.

"If your posture is not correct, your ch'i will tend to be distorted. It will be the same if you train yourself this way while standing up. It will also be the same when you sit facing someone, when you apply yourself to some matter, or even when at work. You should open your chest and shoulders, do not allow your ch'i to become distorted or hindered, and fix your mind so that ch'i will flow fully right to your fingertips.

"Always fix your mind like this, whether bursting forth with your voice while chanting a poem, eating rice, drinking tea, or walking down the road. By doing this, your ch'i will naturally be enlivened on an ordinary basis. When this becomes a constant, you will be quick to respond to unexpected events. If you are indolent in this practice, your ch'i will deaden, and you will be slow to react to any engagement. Being composed and being off-guard may look alike, but they are quite different. You should first test this out for yourself. You may be without literary talent, a beginner, or even a youth, but if you fix your mind in this way, you will accomplish this easily, without great efforts.

"For children rolling a hoop, for the tea ceremony, for *kemari*[58]— for all the lesser arts and the essence of classical dance, too—when ch'i is distorted and has no life, neither the movement nor still-ness of form, nor the continuity of hands and feet will be beautiful. And the performance of action and response will be obstructed.

"When you are forever indolent and mindless, as you grasp your weapon and then suddenly recall that you should have been disciplining yourself in training, your ch'i will change, your mind will be taken by form, and your consciousness will be stopped by your performance. Thus, your ch'i will waver and it will be diffi-cult to respond to unexpected situations.

"If you always use your mind when you train, if an event does occur, you will respond to it with No-Mind. Just always enliven your ch'i, and do not be indolent. Indolent ch'i is dead ch'i. Dead ch'i has no soul. Thus, you will not only be unable to perform any function, but there will be many times when you are startled and made fearful by things.

"When your ch'i fills your entire body and is enlivened together with your mind, there will be neither surprise nor fear, and it will be easy to respond to unexpected changes. Nevertheless, inconstant ch'i has no roots, and does not exist in the truly alive. It appears to, but it is different."

The demon spoke further, "Long ago, a certain Zen monk instructed his acolytes: 'When you pass by a scary place, you should expand your stomach and go right on by. Then you will not be afraid.' This is indeed sound advice. When you expand your stomach, your ch'i drops and gathers at this lower place. For a moment, ch'i will fill you internally and will become strong. When your ch'i is empty and elevated, you will be open to surprise and fear."

The demon continued, "Again, look at someone who is walking. Because most people are usually more conscious of the upper parts of their bodies, they walk counterpoise to their heads, while others walk moving their arms or entire bodies. A person who walks well does not move his body from his waist up, but rather walks with his legs. Thus, his body is serene, his internal organs are not stressed, and he is not worn out. You should observe the manner in which men carry heavy loads.

"When a person who is walking while carrying a sword or halberd has distorted ch'i, he will not be able to move along with

"Again, his ch'i returns to himself, and is not drawn away by whomever he is facing. The person who plays at *kemari* uses his body in the same way."

his feet, and he will damage his body as his arms move about along with his head. His ch'i will move, but his mind will not be at peace. With a sword, the right hand is forward; with a spear, the left. When a person is standing, the foot that will lead off is enlivened.

"You should constantly train yourself in all things, and make great efforts whether walking, sitting, sleeping, or while in contact with other people.

"Look at the way the chief actors in Noh plays use their feet. They all advance while bending the tips of their toes; with feet enlivened, they walk by stepping on their heels. This is not just a matter of carrying themselves elegantly. If the advancing foot is enlivened, the actor will have freedom in using his feet. Again, his ch'i returns to himself, and is not drawn away by whomever he is facing. The person who plays at kemari uses his body in the same way.

"When a skillful Noh actor dances, he will not stumble and fall even when struck from behind. This is because his ch'i is enlivened and fills his entire body: When he moves, the lower half of his body is settled and heavy while the upper half is light, he is in perfect balance, and he speaks breathing from his lower abdomen. When an unskillful man dances, he will stumble and fall over the slightest obstruction. This is because he is light and unsettled below the waist, and his ch'i is distorted and lacking in life: he breathes from above the chest, is lightheaded, and empty below.

"Moreover, when a man skillful at chanting drops his voice to the *ryo* tone,[59] he greatly expands his lower abdomen. You should constantly be trying such things out and knowing them for yourself. Thus, a person who walks along with the lower half of

"When a skillful Noh actor dances, he will not stumble and fall even when struck from behind. This is because his ch'i is enlivened and fills his entire body..."

his body light and the upper half counterpoised will tire quickly.

"These things are endless. When you try fixing your mind on the places you contact with your eyes and ears, you'll find that everything between Heaven and Earth can become the seed of some resourcefulness. There is nothing under Heaven that cannot be said to be your teacher. Everything is important to you, so search it out. When there is absolutely nothing important enough for you to search out, there will be nothing left for you to receive from mankind.

"In a book on strategy, it says, 'When you go out accompanying your master, you should fix your mind on the benefits of what is in front of you, behind you, on your right, on your left, and in the mountains, rivers, and the land.' There were many famous generals in the past who paid great attention to the works of rustic people and, seeing in them the seeds of strategies, performed meritorious deeds. And this is not limited to things military. If you constantly fix your mind on all the Ten Thousand Things in this world, you will gain great benefits. If you are stubborn and empty-headed, you will be no different than a corpse. Whatever there is to gain, you will not be able to grasp it."

One of the group asked, "Military science is the art of deceiving people by means of strategy.[60] If I am mature in the study of this Way, will it not reinforce my superficial knowledge and damage my technique of the mind?"

The demon answered, "When the gentleman uses this, it is an

instrument for the pacification of the state; when the man of little character uses it, it will become an instrument for damaging himself and hurting others. All things are like this. When you set your mind entirely on a Way, if it is not mixed in with self-interest, you could study the technique of being a burglar, but you would use it for the benefit of warding off burglars. This would cause no damage to your intentions. But if your intentions were devoted to passions, desires, greed, profit, and loss, you could study the books of the sages and only encourage your own superficial knowledge. Thus, establish your intentions with the Correct Way of former times, do not alter it, and afterwards study the Ten Thousand Things.

"If you study military techniques without making the Correct Way your mainstay, you will rejoice in clever words, move your mind in their direction, specialize in the skill of superficial knowledge, and make the mistake of considering these to be the Way of the gentleman.

"This is true for the person who studies swordsmanship as well. If a practitioner becomes mature in this art but uses it to try out new swords on passersby or to commit highway robbery, and thinks that this is the Way of a Man, the martial arts will—contrary to what he is thinking—beckon him toward disaster.

"This is not the fault of the martial arts. It is a flaw in one's intentions. Kumasaka and Benkei[61] were both accomplished swordsmen, and both were very strong men endowed with courage and ingenuity. Benkei used these qualities to fight loyally for his master. Kumasaka used them to become a highwayman. Thus, strategy is not in the Way of the gentleman samurai, although *using* it to fight loyally is considered to be that Way. That Benkei struck Yoshitsune with a staff at the Ataka Barrier in Kaga Province was not in itself loyalty. It is considered loyalty because he did it in order to deliver his master from a calamity. One discusses this matter according to its results; it is ignorance to discuss it in terms of the action alone.

"Listen, military strategy is a matter of raising a great number of men, establishing your positions, and making sure that your troops are not destroyed by the enemy. It is the technique of using your own troops and crushing the enemy by using some plan. To use perversity and make propriety the enemy is lawlessness. And would you not damage your own loyal troops with that lawlessness by making no preparations, not using any strategy, fighting improperly, and falling into the enemy's schemes?

"When you *do* have a strategy, you make your preparations ahead of time and do not fall into the enemy's traps. But when you don't understand that technique, you will become the enemy's captive. How could you not understand this?

"Although you could say that there are many techniques to strategies, they are basically used in response to human affections. If the strategy is not in response to human affections, you will not be able to use it, even if you understand its technique. This would be like a doctor reading many books and knowing about the use of many medicines, but not understanding the cause of an illness and applying the medicines arbitrarily. This would likely bring on yet another disease.

"The knowledge of a general is an understanding of human

affections. If a general does not have sincerity, righteousness, and human-heartedness, it will be impossible for him to be in harmony with human affections. It has been clearly understood both in ancient and modern times that when a man does not acknowledge human affections, his strategies will turn into disasters.

"When the enemy runs amok and you abide by the Way, acknowledging human affections will be like having the strength of metal. What would you have to fear of the enemy's strategies? But if the enemy abides by the Way and your troops do not acknowledge human affections, your own strategies will be useless. Thus, the general considers it essential to have a grasp of human affections.

"The educated samurai of today study nothing but the traces of the strategies of famous generals, and this is just the dregs of the ancients. Studying the dregs and coming up with a nutritious soup—this is the measure of a general. For the rank and file, the measure of an educated samurai is to learn a task and then, when the time comes, to perform an action according to that task. Each of the various officers has his own task, and each company has its own methods. Each use of the spear in attack, pause, and retreat has its own function. All of these must be absolutely understood. There have been many great disasters due to an army's smallest mistake in such things as attacking a castle, defending a castle, espionage, night attacks, or entering a territory under the cover of night. When troops face a situation and none know their own part, the consequences can be more deadly than when trying to cross a vast river without knowing how to swim."

Another in the group asked, "If I intend to deceive the enemy with some stratagem, the enemy likely intends to deceive me with some stratagem as well. How could it be that I'm the only man who knows something, while everyone else under Heaven is ignorant?"

The demon replied, "That's exactly it. What you are saying is that people copy set forms. This is like the *go* and *shogi*[62] players who emulated what had come before them, leaving no stone unturned in the principles they had learned. There were no other techniques beyond these. Nevertheless, they were able to become even more skillful than that. To emulate the rules of go or to learn the complex movements of the chessmen in shogi is to study set forms. But once you can freely use these forms, a new and different trick may come out of them that will settle the match.

"Generally speaking, all things in this world appear to be completely like set forms, but this is not so. And strategy is also like this. According to their capacities, generals take from the set forms of the ancients. Then, their actions are adapted to the circumstances and strategies for their troops to spring forth at just the right time. The great generals of the past would observe the skills of fishermen, woodcutters, and men of humble birth, take these directly and create new techniques, many of which were used during campaigns.

"When you constantly keep your mind alert, everything you see and hear becomes an aid to strategies and techniques. Nevertheless, if you do not first know the set forms of the ancients, you will have nothing on which to base your later studies.

"The techniques of Learning are also just like this. If you do not rely on the examples of the ancients, you will be unable to become enlightened in a Way without their examples. You must always use the mind in all things, and consider what your ears hear and your eyes see to be the seeds of discipline. Then, when something happens, you should entrust yourself to the change of that moment.

"Again, during a military campaign, if both your enemies and your allies are made up of large forces, it will be difficult to see things with a freedom as you would in an individual action. Always come up with methods by thinking about the examples of the ancients. It is considered essential to prepare in a way that you will have freedom in moving your troops and leading a cavalry charge.

"Though you have your own good fortune because of the secret acts of charity of your ancestors, when a single thought deviates in the slightest, countless confused minds are generated. In the end, you enter the world of demons, the secret acts of charity of your ancestors are cut off, and disaster comes for you more swiftly than an arrow. All of you should be greatly concerned about this and be very careful about yourselves.

"The world of demons is one where you take pride in your own superficial knowledge, and despise others. You rejoice in the confused actions of others, and by this create the border between good and evil, and gain and loss. You do not know how to enjoy things tranquilly, but—making your own desires absolute—do not reflect on yourself in the least. You consider the person who follows only himself to be good, while you consider it evil to do otherwise. Fastening the world's right and wrong in the fetters of your own egotism, you hate one thing and love the other. At times angry and at times distressd, your mind never enjoys peace and quiet.

"Buddhists call this 'drinking boiling water three times a day and giving birth to flames.' From the suffering of this heat come numerous vicissitudes, perversions, and harm to others. You should all discipline your minds well, control your ch'i, and flee this world of evil spirits. You should enter the world of human beings and search for the Way.

"You all think that because you have long noses, beaks, and wings that you can defeat men and deceive the foolish. Your long noses, sharp beaks, and light wings are instead instruments causing the mind to suffer and men to be injured. In both Learning and swordsmanship, just consider it to be your main business to know yourselves. When you know yourself, you will be clear within and keep yourself well in check. Thus, there will be no reason for anyone to come and be your opponent. Even if your knowledge is insufficient and you make mistakes, it will not be your fault. Just entrust things to Heaven.

"The person who does not know himself does not know others. Those who would deceive and defeat others by means of their own selfish minds will have the vacuity of their minds struck by others. Those who would attack others by means of their own desire will have that desire agitated, and its vacuity struck as well. Those who would overwhelm others by means of force will have the weak point of that force struck, too.

"Learning and swordsmanship are the same. The person without desire who simply exerts everything he has will have no empty space to be struck. Neither can you break him by force. You cannot move him by desire or deceive him with cunning. Thinking of this, I constantly keep myself in check, but still have been unable to cut off my usual common passions. I have simply been able to avoid drinking that boiling water a little. I am still among the ranks of the demons, but will perhaps someday enter the world of men and become enlightened in the Way. I have only briefly explained to you those things I have heard."

The grasses and trees swayed, the mountains rumbled, and this reverberated in the valleys. The swordsman was aware that the wind had picked up. It struck his face and he awoke from a dream. What had appeared to be a mountain was only a folding screen. In great agitation, he fell face down in his bed.

AFTERWORD

I had a guest who criticized this book and said, "What you have discussed here is informed by principle, has the last word on our nature, and is enlightening about the changes of ch'i. But it still does not make the practical application clear. This is fine for the old or infirm, or for cultivating the wills of those who must work diligently. But there are places that are insufficient for someone training in the martial arts."

I said, "I am not a swordsman, so how could I teach people about swordsmanship? It is simply that I've loved the art since I was twenty, and was influenced by martial artists. I asked about the benefits of its techniques, experimented with the transformation of ch'i, and remedied its ailments. I was someone who heard about principle and then sought to prove it to myself with technique of the mind. If from time to time I came to a secret understanding without speaking, I would write it down and show it to others only because of my naivete. I earnestly entreat my friends to pardon me for that quality in myself.

"Nevertheless, I'm afraid that I'm inviting the censure of intelligent people with all these words. Out of necessity, I put this playful discussion into the mouth of a demon. How could I consider this to be anything other than a book about myself talking in my sleep?"

THE DISPATCH

THE MYSTERIOUS TECHNIQUE
OF THE CAT

There was a swordsman by the name of Shoken.[1] One day, a large rat turned up in his house. The rat would not leave, and took to roaming around the house, even in broad daylight. Eventually, Shoken managed to trap the rat in a room, so he could set his cat upon it. But as the cat entered the room, the rat advanced, hurled itself at the cat's face, and sank its teeth into it. The cat let out a scream and ran away. Realizing he was up against more than he had bargained for, Shoken went around the neighborhood and borrowed a number of cats that had made names for themselves as the best of their kind. He chased them into the room where the rat was making its nest in the corner of the alcove, but when one of the cats approached, the rat once again pounced and sank its teeth into it. When the other cats saw this appalling situation, they all fled in fear.

Shoken was outraged and chased the rat about, trying to kill it with a wooden sword he carried at his side, but the rat would slip away and avoid being struck. Furthermore, although all the paper-covered sliding doors were smashed down and torn in the fracas, the rat would jump and escape into the center of the room, always moving with the speed of lightning. It seemed that sooner

When one of the cats approached, the rat once again pounced and sank its teeth into it. When the other cats saw this appalling situation, they all fled in fear.

or later the rat was going to leap at Shoken's face and give him a taste of its teeth. Shoken broke into a sweat and said to himself, "I've heard that not far from here, there is a cat that is first-rate and in fact unequalled. I'd better go borrow that one," and thereupon sent a man off for it.

The cat was brought in and he took a look at it, but it did not appear to be particularly clever or even very active. Still, he thought, "First I'll try putting it into the room anyway," and so he opened the door just a little and put the cat inside. The rat cowered right where it was, and was unable to move. The cat walked over in a leisurely fashion and dragged the rat away as though it were nothing at all.

That night, all the other cats gathered at the house and, inviting the old cat to take the most honored seat, all genuflected before him and, with great respect, said, "We are all called first-rate cats. We have disciplined ourselves in our Way, and sharpen our claws to crush even weasels and otters, not to mention rats. Up to now, however, we have never encountered such a strong rat as this one. Yet you overcame him easily, perhaps by some personal technique. We humbly request that you impart your lordship's mysterious technique to us, holding nothing back."

The old cat laughed and said, "All you young cats work with considerable skill, but you haven't heard about the method of the Correct Way. Thus you have met a situation contrary to your expectations and have come to grief. Nevertheless, I would first like to hear about how each of you have trained."

An agile black cat stepped up from the midst of the group

and said, "I was born into a house of mousers, and have exerted myself in that Way, leaping over seven-foot screens and squeezing myself through tiny holes, so that from the time I was a kitten there was no quick or nimble trick I could not do. Whether it was the strategy of pretending to be asleep or suddenly exploding in a blaze of energy, I never faltered, even with rats that ran along the rafters and beams. But today I have encountered a rat stronger than I could imagine, and have gotten the beating of a lifetime. This is something I never expected."

The old cat said, "Ahh, your discipline is only a performance of skill. Thus, you still haven't escaped from the mind that aims at something. The men of old taught performance in order to inform others of the Way, so such performances were simple and contained a profound principle within them. In these later times, performances of skill are considered specializations: various details are concocted, dexterity is inordinately refined, the ancients' sayings are considered insufficient, and the practitioner uses his own wit and contrivances. In the end, it all comes down to a contest of performance skills; dexterity consumes itself, and for what? Those who practice refining the dexterity of men of little character, and those who specialize in wit and contrivances are all like this. Wit may be used by the mind, but it is not based in the Way. When one specializes solely in dexterity, he is at the edge of make-believe;[2] and, contrary to what you might think, there are many instances of wit and contrivances becoming nothing but drawbacks. You should reflect on such matters in this way, and make great efforts."

Next, a large brindled cat came forward and said, "To my way of thinking, we respect the ch'i[3] of martial arts. Therefore, I have disciplined my ch'i over a long period of time. Now that ch'i is serene and exceedingly strong, and would seem to fill Heaven and Earth. I trample my opponent underfoot, by first defeating him and then advancing. Following the voice, responding to the echo, I control the rat and there is nothing I cannot answer to. I have no thoughts or intentions for using a performance of skill, and my performance flows out on its own. I can just stare at a rat running along the rafters and beams so that it falls off and is taken. Nevertheless, this strong rat has no form when it comes, and leaves no traces when it goes. What kind of thing is this?"

The old cat said, "Your training can only function by depending on the power of ch'i. You are still depending on yourself. This is not the highest good.[4] If you are going out to defeat your opponent, he may also be coming out to defeat you. And what about when defeat turns into no defeat at all? You may disguise your intentions to crush your opponent, but your opponent may do the same. And what about when a disguise turns into no disguise at all? How can it be that only you will be strong and all your opponents weak? Thinking that your ch'i is serene, exceedingly strong, and filling Heaven and Earth, is all just considering its form. It resembles Mencius' 'vast and expansive' ch'i,[5] but in fact it is not. Mencius' ch'i depends on complete clarity and so is strong and sturdy. Yours is strong and sturdy because it depends on power. Thus, their functions are not the same. They are as different as the eternal flow of the Yellow River and the force of an overnight flood. Moreover, when someone will not yield to the energy of your ch'i—what then? There are occasions when a cornered rat will bite a cat, contrary to expectations. Pressed with certain death, there is nothing for it to fall back on. It forgets about life, forgets about its desires, does not consider victory or loss as inevitable, and has no thoughts of preserving its own skin. Thus, its resolve is like iron. How could you defeat an opponent like this with the force of ch'i?"

Then a middle-aged gray cat advanced composedly, and said, "The ch'i of which you speak is fully active, but has a form. Things that have a form may be indistinct, but can be seen. I have disciplined my mind for a long time. I do not develop force, nor do I contend with things. I am in harmony with others, and run counter to nothing. When someone attempts to be tough with me, I meet him with harmony and so become his companion. My technique is like catching pebbles with a large curtain. Though you may speak of a cornered rat, there is nothing to fall back on to contend with me. Nevertheless, today's rat could neither be overcome with force nor met with harmony; both coming and going, he was like a god. I've never seen anything like him up until now."

The old cat said, "Your harmony is not natural harmony. You think, and so create harmony. Though you intend to avoid your opponent's sharp spirit, you still retain a small bit of intention, so your opponent sees through your tactic. If you attempt to reach harmony by inserting your mind, your ch'i will be corrupted and you will be approaching negligence. When you think and then do something, you obstruct your natural perception. And if you obstruct natural perception, how can the mysterious function be given life from anywhere at all? Simply without thinking, without doing anything, move by following your natural perception and your movement will have no form.[6] And when you have no form, there is nothing in Heaven and Earth that could be your opponent.

"That said, each and all of your disciplines are not without value. The meaning of the phrase 'form and spirit are consistent,'[7] is that the highest principle is contained within a performance of technique. Ch'i is what generates function throughout the body. When that ch'i is serene and everywhere, response to things will be boundless; and when you are in harmony, there will be no contending with strength. Though you are struck with metal and rock, you will not be crushed. Nevertheless, even the smallest thoughts will all become [conscious] intentions.[8] This is not the spontaneity[9] of the Way. Thus, when you face off with another, if your mind has not been subdued, the mentality of opposition will exist. What technique will you use then? No-Mind[10] and responding naturally is the only answer.

"Still, the Way is not limited, and you should not think that what I say is the ultimate. Long ago there was a cat in my neighborhood; it slept all day and had no vitality at all. It was like a cat made out of wood.[11] People never saw it catch rats, but wherever the cat was, there were no rats in the vicinity. And this was true even if it changed locations. I went over and asked why this was so, but it gave me no answer. Though I asked it four times, still four times it did not answer.[12] It was not that it could not answer, but that it didn't know what to say. This is, as you know, an example of 'Those who know don't speak; those who speak don't know.'[13] That cat had even forgotten that it had forgotten itself, and had returned to a state of 'Nothingness.'[14] The very spirit of the martial, it killed nothing.[15] I am far and away unable even to approach that cat."

Shoken listened to this as though in a dream. He went over to the old cat, folded his hands over his chest, bowed his head with deep respect, and said, "I have disciplined myself in the art of swordsmanship for a long time, but still have not reached the summit of that Way. Tonight, listening to each of these theories, I have attained the highest degree of my path. May I request that you point out its very deepest mysteries?"

The cat said, "No, I'm just an animal. Rats are my meals. What would I have to do with the actions of human beings? Still, there is something I heard in secret. That is that the art of swordsmanship is not exclusively in making efforts to defeat others. It is the art of dealing with the Great Transformation, and being clear on the matter of life and death. A man who would be a samurai should always maintain this kind of mentality, and should discipline himself in that art. For this reason, you should first of all penetrate the matter of life and death; make no particular adaptations to the mind; have no doubts and no vacillation; do not use your own wit, contrivances, or prejudices; harmonize mind and ch'i; rely on nothing; and be as serene as a deep pool. If you are always like this, you will be completely free to respond to any change.

The cat said ..., "The art of swordsmanship is not exclusively in making efforts to defeat others. It is the art of dealing with the Great Transformation, and being clear on the matter of life and death."

"But when the smallest thing enters your mind, form will appear. And when there is form, there will be an opponent and there will be yourself. Facing each other, there will be conflict; and in a situation like this, the mysterious functions of change and metamorphosis will not occur with freedom. First, your mind will fall into thoughts of death and you will lose all clarity of spirit. How then will you stand readily and with resolve for a fight? Even if you should win, it would be what is called a blind victory, and this is not the true object of the art of swordsmanship.

"'Nothingness' is not what you would call empty-headedness. It is the foundation of the mind and has no form. You should never be taken by phenomena.[16] Once you are the least bit taken by something, your ch'i will be drawn to it. And once your ch'i is even slightly drawn to something, it will be incapable of adaptability or openness. It will go beyond what you are facing, but not reach the place you are not facing. When it goes too far, your energy will overflow and be uncontrollable; when it can't go far enough, it will be clogged up and useless. In neither case will it be able to respond to change. What I am calling 'Not One Thing' means neither being taken by nor drawn toward phenomena, that there is neither opponent nor myself,[17] and that there is nothing more than following phenomena as they come, responding to them, and leaving no traces.

"The *I Ching* says, 'No thoughts, no actions; being serene in non-movement; perceiving and thus becoming intimate with the particulars of Heaven and Earth.'[18] If a man who studies the art of swordsmanship understands this principle, he will be close to the Way."

Shoken asked, "What does 'there is neither my opponent nor myself' mean?"

The cat replied, "Because I exist, my opponent exists. If I do not exist, neither will my opponent. 'Opponent' is the name we give primarily to someone who stands against us. Yin and yang, water and fire, are of this sort. For the most part, something that has form will surely have something in opposition to it. However, if there is no form to my mind, there will be nothing opposing it. When there is nothing in opposition, there is no contention. This is what is meant by 'there is neither an opponent nor myself.' When phenomena and myself have both been forgotten, and I am deeply serene and tranquil, then I am in harmony and at one with the world. Though I crush the form of my opponent, I myself will not know it. This is not 'not knowing,' but rather there will be no thought here whatsoever, and I will only move in accordance with my perceptions. When the mind is deeply serene and tranquil, the world is my world. There is no right and wrong, liking and disliking, or being taken by phenomena. Everything within the boundaries of pain and pleasure or gain and loss are created by my mind. And though we say that Heaven and Earth are vast, there is nothing to seek outside of our own minds.

An ancient worthy said:[19]

> When there is dust in the eye,
>   the three worlds are shut out;
> When the mind and heart are without a care,
>   one's whole life is at ease.

"When even a little bit of dust or sand gets into your eye, your eye is unable to open. And it's just like this when you put something into a bright and clear place where originally there was nothing. This is a metaphor for the mind.

"Another saying has it, 'Surrounded by tens of thousands of the enemy, your form may be pummeled into small pieces, but this mind is still yours. Even the greatest opponent can do nothing about that.' Confucius said, 'Even an ordinary man cannot be robbed of his will.'[20] But when you are confused, that very mind will become an assistant to your opponent.

"I'll stop talking here. You should now simply engage in self-reflection, and seek within yourself. A teacher can only transmit a technique or enlighten you to principle, but receiving the truth of the matter is something within yourself. This is called 'grasping it on one's own.' It is also called 'transmission from mind to mind,'[21] and again, 'a special transmission beyond the scriptures.' This is not turning one's back on the scriptures. It is saying that a teacher cannot transmit this to you. This is not only in the study of Zen. From the 'Law of the Mind' of the Confucian sages down to the arts,[22] 'grasping it on one's own' is always a matter of 'transmission from mind to mind.' It is a 'special transmission' beyond the scriptures. The scriptures are within yourself; [those that are written down] only point out what you have not been able to see on your own.[23] This is not something conferred on you by a teacher. It is easy to teach and also easy to listen to the teachings. It is only difficult to see that they are something within you, and to make them your own. This is called 'seeing into one's own nature.[24] Enlightenment is the perception that you have been having a wild dream. An 'awakening' is the same. There is no difference between them."

AFTERWORD

The setting for *The Demon's Sermon on the Martial Arts* is Mt Kurama, a mountain just north of Kyoto and only 570 meters above sea level, though steep enough to make its ascent a formidable exercise. It is abundant with abrupt cliffs, huge and imposing boulders, and tall dark cyptomerias. In summer, mists suddenly darken its slopes; and even in early winter heavy snow covers the ground, fells trees, and unexpectedly cascades down on the traveler's head when a branch bends or snaps from the weight. In the 11th century, the essayist Sei Shonagon described the path up this mountain as "winding like a vine; nearby, but yet so far away;" and the author of the *Sarashina Nikki*, during the same period, declared that the mountain was so steep that fear kept her from making a pilgrimage there. But if the mountain's terrain was daunting, its mysterious atmosphere was all the more so, for it was known then, as it has been through the ages, as the abode of tengu.

The temple near the mountain's peak, Kurama-dera, was established in 770 A.D. for priests—early precedents of the shugenja—who came to perform mountain austerities. It later became connected with the Tendai sect, and by association, the Shingon sect, the most esoteric sects in Japanese Buddhism. The Honden Kondo, or main temple, is perhaps of average size, but the interior has a strangely cavernous feeling to it, and the visitor senses the same dark atmosphere as of the mountain itself—one appropriate to the transformation of energies and spirit. In the dim light, an elderly priest beats a large drum before the alter and intones one of the many sutras, mantras, or dharanis incorporated in the Tendai teachings. His words are almost totally unintelligible.

In this connection, it is interesting that one of the secret rites practiced by the esoteric sects of Buddhism is meditation on and integration with the Five Dhyana Buddhas, one of whom is called Amoghasiddhi (Jap., Fukujoju, 不空成就), the Buddha of Perfect Power without Obstruction. Amoghasiddhi is visualized as follows: His direction is the north, and his time is midnight. He often rides or is accompanied by garudas, half-men, half-birds that are sometimes confused with tengu. (Both garudas and tengu are considered to be beings in transition to higher states of consciousness and supernatural power, so this uncertainty of identification is not without reason). Amoghasiddhi's color is green, the color of the deep forest, of peace, ease, and nature. His element is air, equal with life-force or ch'i, and he is sometimes depicted moving rapidly through space. In his left hand Amoghasiddhi holds a double vajra, the center of which is a symbol of undifferentiated energy – again, ch'i—which is transformed into spontaneous action, or the of-itself-so: tzu jan.

Amoghasiddhi, above all, unifies the inner and outer worlds, the sacred and the profane. He is, perhaps, the perfect symbol of that liminal world inhabited by both the tengu and the shugenja.

Amoghasiddhi's realm is that of the ashuras, the warring gods so long associated with warriors. His right hand is held upright, palm out in the abhaya mudra, indicating the fearlessness achieved by concentrated meditation on these aspects of his nature, the fearlessness to which all warriors aspire.

The mantra of Amoghasiddhi is "Om amoghasiddhi ah hum."

I sit on a dark wooden bench, trying to make out what the priest is chanting, and wonder if Chozanshi had been aware of these coincidences as well. Can archetypes run that deep? A thin scent of incense penetrates my consciousness and then is gone, and after awhile I am aware that the chanting has stopped and that the temple is silent. In a corner of the temple I purchase some prayer beads and, with a smile, ask the lady if she has ever encountered a tengu here. She shakes her head, answers with an emphatic "Iya, mada desu kedo…"—"No, not yet, but…" and politely retreats to a seat by the kerosene heater. Walking outside into the blinding white snow, I shoulder my rucksack and try to shake off the cold. Dark clouds suddenly cover the small patch of sky again, and I hurry to continue on up the mountain.

ENDNOTES

Preface

1   There are many variations of the Eighteen Martial Arts. Some include a list of weapons such as differing kinds of spears, an iron hammer, the bow, the crossbow, different lengths of swords, etc. Others include takedown techniques such as *tawara* or *jujitsu*, styles of binding an opponent with cords, and even *ninjutsu*.

2   For an interesting summary of some of the more classic styles, see Skoss, Diane, *Classical Warrior Traditions of Japan*, vols. 1 & 2. Koryu Books, Berkeley Heights, 1995 & 1997.

3   Miyamoto Musashi, *The Book of Five Rings*. Tokyo, Kodansha International, 2002, pp. 41, 42.

4   Ibid. p. 122.

5   Heart and mind are written with the same kanji in Japanese: 心.

6   The Sekiyado fief is located in the ancient province of Shimosa; now divided between Chiba and Ibaraki prefectures.

7   Issai Chozanshi (佚斎樗山子). Chozanshi was likely one of the literati, more interested in a quiet life of studying the arts and communing with like-minded friends than in being involved with politics or the great topics of the day. Surely the name he chose as his literary moniker gives us an insight into his personality. The (佚) of Issai can mean to "avoid" (as in society), to "take pleasure in" (as in studies), or to "play around" and "be content." For the Chinese Confucian scholar Mencius, the *Itsudo* (佚道) was the Way of making people happy and at ease. Tellingly, too, the compound (佚遊) means to amuse yourself with your own pursuits. Thus, Issai is the artist who amuses himself and others. Chozanshi, on the other hand, may be taken as the "philosopher of Stinking Tree Mountain." The *cho* (樗)—Ailanthus glandulosa—is a tree known for its twisted and unpleasant-smelling timber.

In the *Chuang Tzu*, when a man complains that the *cho* in his yard is useless, ignored by carpenters and avoided by everyone, Chuang Tzu points out that this precise uselessness is why it has lived so long. He then asks his complaining neighbor, "Why don't you plant it in the village of Nothing-at-All or in the field of Empty-of-Breadth? Knocking about, you could engage in Non-Action at its side; free and easy, you could sprawl out and sleep beneath it. It will not be cut down prematurely by axes great or small, and will be harmed by nothing. Even though it can't be used, how will it ever be troubled or distressed?"

8   See Carmen Blacker, *The Catalpa Bow, A Study of Shamanistic Practices in Japan.* Torquay, The Devonshire Press Ltd., 1975, pp. 181–5.

9   See Yagyu Munenori, *The Life Giving Sword.* Tokyo, Kodansha International, 2003, pp. 66 and 170.

10   Zeami Motokiyo (1363–1443), the father of Noh, heard this rhythm in the cries of insects, the voice of the wind, and even the sound of water.

Introduction

1   The *Nihon Shoki*, the second official history of Japan, completed in 720 A.D. Seng Min's statement was: 流星ニ非ズシテ、是レ天狗ナリ。其ノ吠エル声、雷ニ似タルノミ。

2   Defining or describing tengu is complicated by the fact that in China, tengu had been noted as shooting stars since shortly before the beginning of the first millennium. Further, in the Chinese *Classic of Mountains and Seas* (山海経), also from about that time, a tengu is described as something resembling a black monkey. Interestingly, the Sanskrit term, *ulka*, associated with the kanji for tengu, means simply "meteor;" *ulka-mukha*, or "flaming mouth," refers to the *preta*, the "hungry ghost" who inhabits the Buddhist realm of those born to constant hunger and desire.

3   *Kodama* and *sudama* are spirits born from the ch'i of mountain forests; kodama respond in kind to loud sounds made in the mountains.

4   Kite: *Milvus migrans.* Jap., *tobi.*

5   Even today, there is a common phrase, *Tengu no yatori* (天狗の矢取り), "a tengu catching an arrow in flight," which means something with extreme speed.

6   *Taiheiki*: a fourteenth-century war chronicle.

7   天狗の業を狐は不審に思わず。

8   *Karasu*: Crow. Although tengu are generally described as having the heads of kites, their designation as crow-like has interesting ramifications. Crows are known for their intelligence and also for the mischief they seem to enjoy creating. For an interesting essay postulating that crows have brains developed beyond their physical station, see *Natural Acts* by David Quamman.

9   The phrase *hana ga takai* (鼻が高い) indicates an arrogant or proud person.

10 *Konoha* (木の葉), lit., "tree-leaf," indicating either where they lived or the fans they carried.

11 Traditionally, there are considered to be eight great *konoha* tengu, but the three most famous are Sojobo of Mt. Kurama, Tarobo of Mt. Atago, and Sanshakubo of Mt. Akiba.
    Minamoto Yoshitsune (1159–89) and the swordsman in the *Tengu Geijutsuron* both learned from Sojobo. Kobayakawa Takakage (1533–97) is said to have learned the martial arts from a tengu named Buzenbo living on Mt. Hiko.

12 The term *shungenja* (修験者) simply means "one who practices *shugen.*" The word *yamabushi* (山伏), lit., "one who lies down in the mountains," however, contains a more esoteric meaning, one that the practitioner is recommended to stay in constant meditation. The kanji for mountain (山), for example, is said to symbolize—through its three vertical lines united by a horizontal one—that (1) the three bodies of the Buddha—the *Dharmakaya*, the *Samboghakaya*, and the *Nirmanakaya* are one; (2) the Three Learnings—morality, meditation, and wisdom—are one; and (3) that the mysteries of the Body, Speech, and Mind are one. *Fushi* (伏), on the other hand, gives the radical 人

the meaning of "sacred" (wisdom), united with the radical 犬 meaning (in this case) "attachment," or the "profane." The *yamabushi* is the man who can unite these two, as does the mountain, in one body.

13   Along with the local *kami* and deities (both good and evil), mountains are understood to be the residing places of Dainichi Nyorai, the Universal Buddha; Fudo Myoo, his avatar and messenger, and the major focus of worship of *Shugendo* and other mountain religions; and Zao Gongen, a principle object of *Shugendo,* and perhaps a wrathful manifestation of Shakyamuni, the historical Buddha.

14   While some sects believe that the practitioner absorbs the mountain's ch'i (氣) from this exercise, others report that it is not ch'i, but *rei* (霊), which is variously translated as "spirit" or "soul."

15   The *Genji Monogatari, Utsubo Monogatari, Eika Monogatari, Torikaeba Monogatari, Konjaku Monogatari, Hogen Monogatari, Gempei Monogatari,* and *Taiheiki,* to name just a few.

16   See *The Catalpa Bow,* pp. 184–5.

17   Needham, Joseph. *The Shorter Science and Civilization in China.* Cambridge, Cambridge University Press, 1978, pp. 225–6. Quote translated by Needham.

18   *Tao Te Ching,* Chapter 51.

19   *Lieh Tzu,* 4:10.

20   *Tao Te Ching.* Chapter 76.

21   *Ibid,* Chapter 51.

22   *Ibid,* Chapter 64.

23   Blyth, R.H., *Zen and Zen Classics,* Vol. 1. Tokyo, The Hokuseido Press, 1960, p. 53.

24   *Ibid,* p. 79.

25   Fung Yu-lan, *A History of Chinese Philosophy,* Vol. 1, Princeton, Princeton University Press, 1973, p. 155. This quote translated by Fung Yu-lan.

26 *Chuang Tzu*, 7:16.

27 "Happy excursion" and "free and easy wandering" are translations of these three kanji, by Fung Yu-lan and Burton Watson, respectively.

28 *Tao Te Ching*, Chapter 2.

29 *The Unfettered Mind*, p. 49.

30 Jiang Lansheng, ed., *One Hundred Excerpts from Zen Buddhist Texts*. Hong Kong, Shang Wu Yin Shu Kuan, 1997.

THE DISCOURSES

Transformation of the Sparrow and the Butterfly

1 Previous form. (俗姓 *zokusho*). Lit., the name of a priest or monk before taking the tonsure.

2 This according to ancient Chinese folklore, possibly based on the gathering of sparrows at the seashore around the month of September.

3 In the Taoist work, *Chuang Tzu*, from around the 4th cent. B.C.

4 *Nembutsu*. Recitation of the phrase, *Namu Amida Butsu* (Homage to Amida Buddha). The Pure Land sects believe that recitation of this phrase with true sincerity and feeling will bring one to rebirth in Amida's Western Paradise.

5 Becoming a Buddha (成仏 *jobutsu*). Literally meaning "becoming a Buddha," it is also a phrase that simply means "to die," as Westerners might say "He went to Heaven."

6 This again according to ancient Chinese folklore. In section 24 of the *Ts'ai Ken T'an* (Vegetable Root Discourses by Hung Ying-ming, 17th cent.), we read:
> The vermin that crawl through the dung are the extremity of filth,
> But transformed, they become cicadas drinking dew in the autumn wind.

Rotten grass has no light,
But it metamorphoses and becomes the fireflies that shine with
iridescence under the summer moon.

The Owl's Understanding

1   This is the *mimizuku* or *washimimizuku* in Japanese. It is called the
    eagle owl in English, and bears the charming latin name of *Bubo
    bubo*. It seems to be very rarely seen in Japan, but Chozanshi may
    have confused it with other horned owls ("eared" in Japan), particu-
    larly with the *torafuzuku* or long-eared owl (Latin: *Asio otus*), which is
    much more common.

2   The outfit of a *yamabushi*, a priest of an esoteric sect in Japan. They
    wander the mountains, and are considered by some to be frightening.

3   Tengu: A mythical creature with a long nose, able to fly by means of
    a palm frond.

4   Owls are included among the hawks in Japan. The name itself, *washi-
    mimizuku*, means "eagle owl," or "eagle with ears attached."

5   "What Heaven commands is called our nature. (天性)" *Doctrine of the
    Mean*.

6   Chogenbo: A kind of hawk, also called the "horse dung hawk," or
    more simply the "dung hawk." This is the Eurasian kestral in English
    (Latin: *Falco tinnun-culus*). It is commonly seen in Japan during the
    winter.

7   Lao Tzu: Presumed author of the *Tao Te Ching*, and as such, the
    founder of Taoism.

The Seagull and the Mayfly Discuss the Tao

1   Two animals generally considered to be symbols of long life in the
    Far East.

2   The Great P'eng: A huge mythological bird that beats its wings and

creates a whirlwind. It begins life as a monstrous fish called the Kun, but later changes into a P'eng.

3   One *ri* equals 2.44 miles.

4   The four great elements (四大仮合). A Buddhist term; the four great elements are earth, water, fire, and wind.

5   Shaba. The Buddhist term used to describe this painful world. Among the many etymologies of this word, one of the most interesting is the one that states the meaning to be contained within the image of a rosebush. The rose is beautiful, but you will be pricked by its thorns if you try to pick it.

6   *Kunshi.* The Confucian gentleman, or a princely, well-educated man.

7   Without attachment (無心 *mushin*). This term could also be translated as "mindlessly," but is often given as "No-Mind" by Zennists.

Profit and Loss for the Bulbul and the Wren

1   The Brown-eared Bulbul (*Hypsipetes amaurotis*). Gregarious and noisy.

2   Heavenly Bamboo (*Nandina domestica*).

3   Also called the Winter Wren (*Troglodytes troglodytes*). One of the smallest birds in Japan, but with a loud and elaborate song.

4   A point stressed a number of times by Miyamoto Musashi in *The Book of Five Rings*.

The Centipede Questions the Snake

1   The readings required of every Confucian scholar. The Four Books are: *The Analects, The Great Learning,* the *Doctrine of the Mean,* and the *Mencius.* The Six Classics are: *The Book of Odes, The Book of History, The Book of Rites, The Book of Changes, The Rites of Chou,* and *The Spring and Autumn Annals.*

2   In ancient times, earthworms were considered to be able to sing.

3   Yellow Springs: It is noted that here the term simply means "underground wells," but traditionally it has meant the place we go when we die.

4   P'eng Tsu: The Methuselah of China.

The Skills of the Heron and the Crow

1   The word here is *fumu*, which ordinarily means "to step on," while a secondary meaning is "to take." Chozanshi is apparently making a sort of pun here, extended in the next note.

2   The *dojo* (鰌) is a mudfish or loach (*Misgurmus anguillicandatus*). *Dojo* (土壤), however, means "soil," so one is left with a heron either taking mudfish, stepping on soil, or perhaps stepping on mudfish. It is left to the reader.

3   *Nyoro-nyoro*: To wriggle along something like a snake. This is onomatopoeia, and usually written in the Japanese kana or phonetic alphabet, but Chozanshi writes it here using the Chinese characters for "like" (如) and "heron" (鷺), which together happen to be pronounced *nyoro*.

4   Crows have been considered omens of bad luck since ancient times in the Far East.

5   Thatched huts, of course.

6   *Hyla arborea*

7   同声相応 同気相求. A phrase from the *I Ching*.

The Toad's Way of the Gods

1   According to Japanese folktales, when a cat reaches an advanced age, it turns into a huge monster with the eyes of a cat and the body of a dog, and is called a *nekomata*. It lives deep in the mountains and

devours passersby, usually at night. In section 89 of the 12th century classic *Tsurezuregusa*, by Yoshida Kenko, we read, "Deep in the mountains there are creatures called *nekomata* that eat people."

2 See above. *The Skills of the Heron and the Crow*, note 7.

3 From Chapt. 4 of the *Tao Te Ching*: "The Tao…dulls sharp edges, unravels entanglements, softens bright lights, and becomes one with the dust." 挫其鋭, 解其紛, 和其光, 同其塵. It may be interesting to see other translations of this very germinal phrase of the book. James Legge reads it as: "We should blunt our sharp points, and unravel the complications of things; we should attemper [sic] our brightness, and bring ourselves into agreement with the obscurity of others." Red Pine gives it a slightly different angle: "…dulling our edges, untying our tangles, softening our light, merging our dust…"

The Greatest Joys of the Cicada and Its Cast-off Shell

1 Although there are probably more than thirty-five different kinds of cicadas in Japan, we can generally reduce them to two types: the kind that spends seven years underground as a grub, and then emerges to shed its shell and live a few weeks as a cicada, and the kind that spends an astonishing fourteen years underground and emerges to the same fate. In Japan the grubs usually emerge in late August or early September, climb part of the way up a tree, and then break out of the back or bottom of the shell, leaving it behind, attached to the tree. Their cries, usually given the sound *min min* or *tsuku tsuku*, depending on the species or sub-species, are described in haiku as being able to penetrate rocks. In one of his essays, Lafcadio Hearn informs us that "…the reader may be surprised that out of [cicada]-skins there used to be made in both China and Japan—perhaps upon homeopathic principles—a medicine for the cure of earache!" In Chinese mythology, the cicada is considered a symbol of rebirth or immortality.

2 *Itamu* (痛む) means to experience pain or to be hurt, while *itamu* (悼む) means to grieve over or to bemoan something, so the homonym provides Chozan with a pun that is meaningful either way it is read.

3   I.e., If I have no enterprises, I will not have their concomitant worries
     either.

4   *Jakumetsu iraku* (寂滅爲楽). *Jakumetsu* means tranquil and extin-
     guished: the tranquil state of complete extinction of passions and
     cycles of birth and death. In other words, Nirvana. *Iraku* is literally
     "making joy."

5   I.e., from sins, passions, and worldly cares.

6   A common expression in the Orient for the lack of worldly attach-
     ments or possessions. Someone who can drink only the dew has not
     only material poverty, but spiritual poverty as well. He or she is free
     from (almost) everything.

The Dream of the Cucumber

1   Lit., "shouldering a mountain." This seems to be taken from a line in
     the *Chuang Tzu* concerning the futility of having a mosquito shoul-
     der a mountain.

2   The day after Obon, the Feast of Lanterns, or the Festival of the Dead.
     Traditionally, the spirits of the departed are invited back to their old
     homes, entertained with dancing, music, and offerings of food and
     sake, and then sent off back to their resting places with small floating
     lanterns

3   Cucumber: This is given variously as the *nauri*, the *shirouri*, and the
     asauri, but seems to be what we call a melon cucumber in English. It
     is described as being greenish-white, and is perhaps a bit larger than
     the cucumbers we buy in stores. I have been unable to find its Latin
     designation.

4   Such items were carved and set on a special "spirit shelf" used for the
     Obon festival.

5   A kind of salad made with salt, vinegar, and finely chopped cucum-
     ber; or possibly a sort of white cucumber.

6   A salad made with finely sliced fish, vegetables, vinegar, and miso.

7   A fish and vegetable salad topped with vinegar.

8   Pickles seasoned in sake lees.

The Ghost at the Old Temple

1   For Fuzan, see above: *The Dream of the Cucumber*.

2   Kanto: Literally, "East of the Barrier." This first referred to those prov-
     inces east of the Osaka Barrier, but later came to mean those east of
     the Hakone Barrier.

3   Humanity (仁) is considered to be at the very core of Confucian
     thinking. It concerns the way people act, one toward another. Taoism
     pointed out that a humanity-based philosophy ignored man's inti-
     mate connection with the rest of the world, and somehow missed
     the fact that man is not the center of the universe.

4   無為: The great Taoist and Buddhist concept of Inactivity, or not fuss-
     ing with the world. It indicates the spontaneous and natural, rather
     than something done with a purpose in mind, and implies that
     which is free from the passions and attachment. It is the dharma-
     nature of all things, which we constantly mess up with our plans and
     schemes. 為無為 is "Doing without doing," the Taoist and Buddhist
     ideal and something beyond the Confucian ken.

Meeting the Gods of Poverty in a Dream

1   Daikokuten: One of the Seven Gods of Good Fortune. Usually
     depicted as a smiling, fat (or at least robust) man carrying a large bag
     filled with blessings over his left shoulder, and carrying a mallet with
     which he beats out good fortune in his right hand. He stands atop
     two rice bales and is often accompanied by mice, which are his mes-
     sengers. In India, he was Mahakala, a fierce manifestation Kannon
     and a protector of Buddhism; and in Japan is often conflated with
     Okuni-nushi, a mythological founder of the country. He became one
     of the Seven Gods of Good Fortune around the early 17th century,

and is considered one of the "kitchen gods" along with his companion, Ebisu.

2 The Seven Gods of Good Fortune (*Shichifukujin*): Said to bring luck and good wealth. Formed from the Chinese model in the late 16th or early 17th century, this group quickly became an object of veneration by the common people. This combination of gods mixes Indian, Chinese, and Japanese divinities symbolizing for the Confucians the seven human virtues: longevity, luck, popularity, candor, kindness, dignity, and magnanimity. The phrase, however, is also said to be derived from the Buddhist term, "the seven disasters and the seven good fortunes," which are different according to the source. They are often depicted in a group, sailing together on the *Takarabune*, or Ship of Treasures, and this image is considered a powerful charm. Besides Daikokuten (see above), they are:

- Ebisu, the god of work, health, and prosperity, and possibly the son of Daikokuten. He is depicted with a large fish under one arm, probably of Japanese origin, and is venerated by fisherman and tradespeople;

- Bishamonten, an armed warrior of Indian origin, who protects Buddhism;

- Benzaiten, of Indian origin, a goddess of the arts, love, and music, usually depicted carrying a lute;

- Fukurokuju, a god of wisdom, virility, fertility, and longevity; of Chinese origin, and portrayed as an old bearded man with a head three times as big as his body—sometimes in a phallic shape;

- Jurojin, a god of longevity of Chinese origin, portrayed as an old man leaning on a long stick and accompanied by a crane;

- Hotei, a 10th-century eccentric Korean monk who lived in China, but is also considered an incarnation of Maitreya, the Buddha of the future; worshipped as a god of good fortune, he is depicted as fat, almost always smiling (he is sometimes yawning, while waiting to be reborn as a Buddha some millions of years from now), and carrying a bag filled with blessings, which he generously distributes.

3   *Hitoyogiri*: A flute made from a single piece of bamboo, slightly shorter than a *shakuhachi*.

4   Yao and Shun (2333–2234 B.C. and 2233–2184 B.C. respectively): Legendary wise rulers of China, who ruled by virtue rather than by military threat. In *The Book of Lu Pu-wei*, it states, "Yao had ten sons, but he passed them over and made Shun his successor. Shun had nine sons, but he passed them over and made Yu his successor." (Renditions, Nos. 33 & 34—Spring and Autumn 1990.)

5   - Ch'ao Fu: A hermit who lived during the age of Yao and Shun. He lived away from the vulgar world and slept in the top of a tree, thus his name, "Nest Father (巢父)."

    - Hsu Yu: Another virtuous man of the same period. When Shun offered him the throne, he retreated to the mountains and washed out his ears in a clear stream to purify them from the contaminated words that had just entered them. When a nearby hermit heard of this, he led his cow upstream to cleaner water.

    - Yen Yuan (Yen Hui): Of all the disciples of Confucius, the one most fond of learning, and the only one who would "know ten after hearing one." It was Yen Yuan of whom the Master spoke, "Admirable indeed was the virtue of Hui! With a single bamboo dish, a gourd for a cup, and living in a narrow lane, while others could not have endured the distress, he did not allow his joy to be affected by it."

    - Min Tze Ch'ien: Distinguished for his virtuous principles and practice, and for his filial piety. Mencius said that Min had "all parts of the sage, but in small portions." (Mencius, Bk II, pt.1. Chapt. II). He refused office when it was offered, and threatened to go and live by the bank of a river. He is described as "standing by the Master, looking introspective." (Analects, Bk 11, chapt. 13.)

    - Yuan Hsien: A disciple of Confucius said to have lived in pure poverty.

6   See the above note, viz. Yen Yuan. (Analects, Bk 6, Chapt. 11.)

7   The meal offered to Daikokuten on his festival day.

8   Gaki (餓鬼): The inhabitants of one of the low realms of reincarnation (there are six realms in all) according to Buddhist tradition. In their former lives as human beings, they were avaricious and greedy. Gaki are always hungry, but have very thin necks and distended bellies, and so can eat only a little at a time, and are never satiated.

9   Ou Yang: Possibly Ou Yang-hsiu (1007–72), a scholar of the Northern Sung Period who attempted to revive the old style of literature. He emphasized that writers should be free to express their ideas in whatever form they liked.

10   Human-heartedness (仁): A concept at the very center of Confucian ideals. The Chinese character shows a human being and the number 2, indicating how people should interact. According to Wing-Tsit Chan, it has been translated variously as "benevolence, perfect virtue, human-heartedness, love, altruism," etc. It is the basis of all goodness. Mencius (6A, 11) calls it 'man's mind.' Neo-Confucianists interpreted it as impartiality, the character of production and reproduction, consciousness, the will to grow, and one who forms one body with Heaven and Earth."

11   Yen Tze-lu. Another name for Yen Yuan.

12   Ch'i Chang-k'ai: A disciple of Confucius. Encouraged by the Master to become a public servant, he declined, stating his lack of self-confidence. Praised by Confucius for his character.

THE SERMON

1   Death-dealing sword and Life-giving sword: Concepts developed in the Yagyu Shinkage-ryu of swordsmanship by Yagyu Sekishusai and his son Yagyu Munenori. According to the Shinkage-ryu, if the sword is held in a stance, it is called the Death-dealing sword, or *satsujin-to*. If it is not held in a stance, it is termed the Life-giving sword, or *katsujinken*. The purpose of the Death-dealing sword is to

cut down the opposition; that of the Life-giving sword is to give life to the opposition. Furthermore, the Life-giving sword, not being held in a stance, tends to provoke the opposition to action, thus "giving life" or "activity" to the opponent's sword. See *The Life-Giving Sword* by Yagyu Munenori.

2   Kanda Hakuryushi: During the middle and late Edo period, there was a series of professional storytellers using the family name Kanda (神田), and the character *haku* (伯) as part of their personal names. Was Kanda Haukuryushi one of these men? Neither his dates nor the circumstances of his life are clear. As Chozanshi himself was a great storyteller in writing, Hakuryushi may well have been a friend with like-minded interests.

3   A moving being (動物): The characters together mean "animal," but the literal meaning is "moving thing, or creature."

4   Study of the mind, or mind technique (心術).

5   The Six Arts: The Six Arts of the Confucian gentleman—ceremonies, music, archery, carriage-driving, writing, and mathematics.

6   Mind considered fundamental: "In archery, we do not consider the target as fundamental. This is because our strengths are not the same. This is the Way of the ancients." *Analects*: 3,16.

7   *Analects*, 15,29. It is man who makes the Way great, not the Way that makes man great.

8   Minamoto Yoshitsune/Ushiwakamaru (1159–89): Great hero of the Genpei conflicts. Renowned for his martial prowess, which was supposedly learned from *tengu*. In his youth he was called Ushiwakamaru.

9   Mt. Kurama: A mountain (570 m.) just north of Kyoto, known for its mysterious atmosphere. Long considered the lair of *tengu*.

10   Kumasaka Chohan: A famous bandit of the Heian period (794–1192). He was supposedly killed by the young Yoshitsune in 1117. Another theory has it that he suddenly "got religion" as he climbed Mt. Koya on his way to a planned robbery, broke out his own front teeth, erected an ossuary, and disappeared leaving only a poem behind.

11 The Hua Yen (Japanese *Kegon*) Buddhist assertion that only the material can manifest Emptiness.

12 Great Ultimate (太極): According to the Neo-Confucian school, the Great Ultimate exists before anything else. It gives rise to yin and yang, which in turn beget the Five Elements (Water, Earth, Wood, Fire, Metal), which then in turn give the world its multitudinous forms.

The Great Ultimate through movement generates yang. When its activity reaches its limit, it becomes tranquil. Through tranquility the Great Ultimate generates yin. When tranquility reaches its limit, activity begins again. So movement and tranquility alternate and become the root of each other, giving rise to the distinction of yin and yang, and the two odes are thus established.

By the transformation of yang and its union with yin, the Five Agents of Water, Fire, Wood, Metal, and Earth arise. When these five material forces (ch'i) are distributed in harmonious order, the four seasons run their course.

Chou Tun-I in *A Source Book in Chinese Philosophy*,
By Wing-Tsit Chan, p. 463.

13 Four Fundamental Virtues: Humanity, righteousness, propriety, and wisdom.

14 Training: This word also defines the training of Buddhist priests, and implies the same level of ascetic practices.

15 Abiding in the midst of attack, attacking in the midst of abiding. See *The Life-Giving Sword*, Yagyu Munenori, pp. 78–79.

16 Emphasizing the need for precision and clarity.

17 That Way, i.e., the Way of Archery.

18 *Great Learning*: One of the four most important books of Confucian learning. The Chinese is: 大学之道, 在明明德, the meaning of which has been argued for centuries.

19 *Doctrine of the Mean*: Another of the Four Confucian Books. The full phrase is "What is commanded by Heaven is called [our] nature. To follow [our] nature is called the Way. To practice the Way is called education."

20 Phrases found in the *Great Learning*, although one quote has been slightly changed. The Confucian text has it: "Making one's mind correct, and making one's will sincere."

21 From the *Doctrine of the Mean*: "Therefore the gentleman watches himself carefully when alone."

22 Compare this with Takuan in the *Taiaki*: "The enemy does not see me. I do not see the enemy." See *The Unfettered Mind*, by Takuan Osho, p. 112.

23 Tzu Lu: A disciple of Confucius known for his courage, and often mentioned in the 10th section of the *Analects*. In *The Doctrine of the Mean* there is the following:

> Tzu-lu asked about strength. The master said, "The strength of the South or the strength of the North? Or perhaps do you mean your own strength? To teach by being composed and gentle, and to not retaliate against outrageous conduct is the strength of the South. The gentleman resides in this. To make one's bed of weapons and armor and not to begrudge death is the strength of the North. The strong man resides in this. Therefore, the gentleman lives in harmony but does not run along with the current. His strength is straight and true! He stands at the center and does not recline. His strength is straight and true!

24 *The Analects*: 4, 8:
The Master said, "If [a student] is not excited [about a subject], I do not instruct him. If I raise a single corner and express something, and he does not come back by raising three, I do not repeat myself."

25 *Tao Te Ching*, Chapt. 64: "Act on things before they exist."

26 *Tao Te Ching*, Chapt. 27: "Good traveling leaves no tracks or traces."

27 Great Vitality (大体気): The ch'i that envelopes and permeates the physical world.

28 *Lieh Tzu*, Chapt. 2:
> "Being single-minded, nothing will stand against you."
> "When you gamble for tiles, you are skillful. When you gamble for your belt buckle, you begin to hesitate; and when you

gamble for gold, you get confused. Your skill is the same, but you get cautious because you value something outside yourself. When you do this you become awkward inside."

29 *Chuang Tzu*, Chapt. 15:
[The wise man] avoids knowledge and personal motives, but follows the principles of Heaven. Thus, there are no disasters from Heaven, no obstructions from things, and no censure from man. Life is like floating, death is like a rest.

30 *Mencius*: 10, 3. These activities were thought to be very important for social order and justice. Mencius was the greatest writer on Confucianism after Confucius himself.

31 *The Book of Rites*: "Rites, music, punishments, and laws are all—at their extreme—one."

32 *Tao Te Ching*, Chapt. 29:

The man who acts [through the will] harms it; the man who grasps it loses it.

33 Hoka (放下): A man dressed as a Zen priest beating *kogiriko* (beans contained in a bamboo pipe)—one in each hand—while dancing and singing.

34 *Lieh Tzu*, Chapt. 1:
For this reason, the Way of Heaven and Earth, if not yin, will be yang; the proper function of the Ten Thousand Things, if not soft, will be hard. All of these follow their proper functions, and are unable to leave their stations.

35 *Chuang Tzu*, Chapt. 24:
You must make your will one. Don't listen to things with your ears. Listen to things with your mind. Don't listen to things with your mind, listen to them with your ch'i. Listening stops in the ears; the mind stops in phenomena.

36 *Chuang Tzu*, Chapt. 19:
Confucius was sight-seeing in Lu-liang. There was a place where the water plummeted thirty fathoms, then flowed and bubbled and splashed along for another forty *li*, so that neither fishes nor water

creatures could swim there. He noticed a man swimming in just that spot, and so thought the man was suffering some pain and wanted to die. He ordered his disciples to line up along the current and to rescue the man. But after a few hundred paces, the man got out on his own and walked leisurely along the embankment, letting his hair fall where it might and singing a song as he went. Confucius followed along after him and asked, "I took you for a demon, now I realize you are a man. I would like to ask if you have some Way of treading the water." The man said, "No, I have no Way at all. I start with my beginnings, grow with my character, and complete things with my destiny. I enter along with the whirlpools, and come out where it's calm; I follow the Way of the water, and do not consider myself. For this reason, I'm able to tread along." Confucius said, "What do you mean when you say, 'I start with my beginnings, grow with my character, and complete things with my destiny'?" The man said, "I was born on the land and felt repose on the land, this was my beginnings. I grew up in the water and felt repose in the water. This is my character. Not knowing why, I naturally do what I do. This is my destiny."

37   See the *Taiaki* in *The Unfettered Mind*, p. 112.

38   *Tao Te Ching*, Chapt. 63:
Act with no action; use the technique of no technique.

39   *Tao Te Ching*, Chapts. 2, 10, 51:
He acts, but does not rely [on anything].

40   *Chuang Tzu*, Chapt. 8:
When I speak of a master, it is not a matter of human-heartedness or righteousness. It is being a master of your own particular virtue... It is a matter of following the conditions of your own given nature.

41   *Tao Te Ching*, Chapt. 37:
All things will be transformed of themselves.

42   *Tao Te Ching*, Chapt. 81:
The Way of the sage is to act, but not contend.

43   I.e., Your everyday life will aid and cultivate your art, and your art will aid and cultivate your everyday life.

44 *Lieh Tzu*, Chapt. 2:
Confucius said, "Don't you know? The man with absolute sincerity can affect things. He moves Heaven and Earth, influences gods and demons, traverses the six cardinal points, and nothing opposes him."

45 *The Analects*: 9,12. Tze-Yu said, "The young disciples of Tze-hsia were good at sprinkling the ground and sweeping up, answering and responding, and coming forward and taking leave. But these are only the branches."

46 *Chuang Tzu*, Chapt. 7:
The man who has arrived uses his mind like a mirror. He does not chase after things, neither does he invite them.

47 Sutoku: 75th Emperor of Japan (1119–64).

48 *The Life-Giving Sword*, p. 108: The moon moves its reflection to the water with remarkable immediacy. Though it may be high up in the distant sky, its reflection pieces the water as soon as the clouds move aside. This is not something that comes down from the Heavens gradually or by degrees and then is reflected. It is reflected faster than you can blink your eyes.

49 *Zanshin* (残心): Something remaining in the mind; a mental attachment to an action already completed. In swordsmanship, zanshin can refer either to the above, or to a mental preparation for a reaction from an opponent at whom you have just struck. In archery it may mean retaining a tension while discerning a reaction from a released string.

50 "Taking the initiative is surely at the heart of taking the victory." See *The Book of Five Rings* by Miyamoto Musashi, p. 100.

51 "The mind is the soul of ch'i." The Chinese character for "soul" (霊) has a number of meanings, including soul, priestess, spirit, ghost, or even a deceased person's memory. It originally indicated priestesses or shamanesses praying for rain, and should not be too closely thought of in our own Western terms.

52 *Lieh Tzu*, Chapt. 1:
The pure and light rise and become Heaven. The muddy and heavy

descend and become Earth. The ch'i that comes together in harmony becomes man.

53   When Ch'ao Fu was offered the throne by Yao, he washed his ears in a stream to clean them out. When Hsu Yu heard about this, he led his cow upstream so it would not drink contaminated water.

54   Chuang Tzu's *Discussion on Swords*. This is a Taoist treatise on the administration of the state, and has little to do with the martial arts.

55   Chuang Tzu's *Mastering Life*. A short section in this chapter relates the following:

> Chi Hsing-tzu was keeping fighting cocks for the king. Ten days went by and the king asked, "Are the cocks ready yet?"
> Chi replied, "Not yet. They're still too fierce and reliant on temper."
> After ten more days, the king inquired again.
> Chi replied, "Not yet. They still react to sounds and everything around them."
> After ten more days, the king inquired again.
> Chi replied, "Not yet. They still glare at other cocks, and have too much fighting spirit."
> After ten more days, the king inquired again.
> Chi replied, "Just about! Another cock may crow, but these don't change at all. Look at them from a distance, and they resemble cocks made of wood! The characteristic [you're looking for] is complete. Other cocks will not dare to be their opponents, but will show their tails and run."

56   The hook spear (*kagiyari*): A spear with a cross-shaped hook at the neck of the shaft. Generally used to twist away the opponent's weapon.

The tube spear (*kudayari*): A kind of spear used during the Edo period. The shaft of the spear is enclosed in a short tube, which is held in the left hand. The spear is thrust out and withdrawn by the right hand. A ring is fitted around the shaft near the neck of the spear to keep it from being withdrawn too far into the tube.

57   Suzuki Shozan (1579–1655): More often pronounced Suzuki Shosan, Served both Tokugawa Ieyasu and Hidetada with brave deeds on the

battlefield, then shaved his head and studied Buddhism. The Nio are the two Vajrapani (Diamond-hand) kings whose statues often stand at the entrance of Buddhist temples to scare off the enemies of Buddhism (our greed, anger, and ignorance).

58 *Kemari*: Japanese court football.

59 *Ryo* (呂). The lowest tone of those used in chanting.

60 Compare with "Deception is strategy." Yagyu Munenori in *The Life-Giving Sword*, p. 76. Or with Sun Tzu's famous line, "Warfare is the Way of deception." (兵者詭道也).

61 Yoshitsune was being pursued by the armies of his brother Yoritomo, and had disguised himself as Benkei's servant. When the guard at Ataka became suspicious, Benkei struck Yoshitsune to convince the guard that Yoshitsune was indeed a servant, and not the famous general he actually was.

62 *Go* and *shogi*: Two Oriental board games. *Shogi* is somewhat similar to Western chess, but *go* is played on a more extensive field, and uses black and white stones. The object of *shogi* is to capture the opponent's men, while the object of *go* is more to capture territory.

THE DISPATCH

The Mysterious Technique of the Cat

1 Shoken (勝軒): *Sho* means "victory" or "victorious," while *ken* usually means "eaves." Nevertheless, it can also mean "dancing" or "laughter"—both good Taoist subjects—and "being good at" or "making a specialty of," which seems most likely here. *Ken* is also a homonym with "sword."

2 From Lao Tzu's *Tao Te Ching*, section 57: "When man makes a great deal of skill and cunning, off-beat ways arise more and more." Chozan's word "make-believe" also can mean "falsehood." Both meanings—one directed inwardly, the other outwardly—are appropriate.

3   Ch'i: The vitality that is the very foundation of the body.

4   *Tao Te Ching*, section 8: The highest good is like water; it benefits the Ten Thousand Things, but does not contend with them.

5   *The Mencius*: "Again he asked, 'What is this broad and expansive ch'i?' He said, 'It's difficult to say. It is extremely great and strong, and because of this it nurtures and does not harm. Thus it fills the space between Heaven and Earth.'"

6   *I Ching, The Commentaries*: "Change does not think, it does not act [with intent]. It is serene and does not move. It perceives and thus penetrates everything under Heaven." Note that "change" (易) can also be read as "easy."

7   Lit., The utensil and the Way are consistent. The meaning is that the manifest is the utensil, and the spirit within is the Way. *I Ching, The Commentaries*: "With form, the ascendant is called the Way, while the descendant is called the utensil."

8   *Sakui* (作意), intention, is a homonym of *sakui* (作為), artificiality.

9   *Shizen* (自然): Lit., "of-itself-so," means both the natural world (which includes ourselves) and its internal laws. Spontaneity (see introduction).

10 *Mushin* (無心): The Zen Buddhist ideal—a mind without calculations, prejudices or pre-valuing. Lit., "no mind." It is the mind empty of all artifice, completely open to whatever enters it. It reflects the manifest world like a mirror, without the distortion of ideas of right and wrong, gain and loss, or attraction and repulsion. It is the enlightened mind.

11 This refers to the story in the *Chuang Tzu* of a man who trained gamecocks. He declared that any outward manifestation of energy, ferocity, or reaction to things about them indicated that the cocks were not yet trained to the highest degree. It was only when "you look at them and they resemble cocks made of wood," that their discipline and training are complete. (See note 55 in *The Sermon*.)

12 *Chuang Tzu*: Nieh Ch'ueh was trying to question Wang Ni: "Four times he asked him, and four times he simply said, 'I don't know.'"

13 *Tao Te Ching*, section 56: "The one who knows does not speak; the one who speaks does not know."

14 *Tao Te Ching*, section 14: "Continuous and consistent, it cannot be given a name. It returns again to Nothingness." This *mubutsu* (無物), traditionally translated as "Nothingness" in Taoist texts, is the great source of everything in the universe. Chozan, however, seems to mix its meaning with the Zen Buddhist *Mu Ichi Motsu* (無一物), meaning that not one thing exists on its own, that everything is contingent on other things—Nothingness with a slightly different twist. Thus we should not, and indeed cannot, rely on anything. Rather, we should always return to the boundless source of Nothingness.

15 *I Ching, The Commentaries*: "The wise and sagacious men of ancient times had the very spirit of the martial and did not kill."

16 In the *Fudochishinmyoroku*, the Zen priest Takuan (1573–1645) emphasized that the mind of a swordsman should not be taken (stopped or moved) by anything at all. If it were to be taken, its free-flow would be clogged up and the unfettered movement of both body and mind would be arrested.

17 In the *Taiaki*, also by Takuan, we read: "Presumably, as a martial artist, I do not fight for gain or loss, am not concerned with strength or weakness, and neither advance a step nor retreat a step. The enemy does not see me. I do not see the enemy. Penetrating to a place where Heaven and Earth have not yet divided, where yin and yang have not yet arrived, I quickly and necessarily gain effect."

18 See note 7.

19 Referring to a poem by the Zen priest Muso Kokushi (1275–1351). The full verse runs:

> How many times have the green mountains turned to yellow
> The vigorous confusion of this world never ends.
> A speck of dust gets in your eye and the Three Worlds are closed up.
> But if there is nothing in your mind, all about you is broad and wide.

20   *The Analects*, 5:26: "A great army can be robbed of its general, but even a common man cannot be robbed of his will."

21   *Ishin denshin* (以心伝心): A Zen Buddhist phrase meaning that the transmission of the enlightened mind does not rely upon words or texts. In *The Bloodstream Sermon*, Bodhidharma states, "In the arising of the Three Worlds, they all return to the One Mind. Both Buddhas in the past and Buddhas in the future transmit mind with the mind. They do not stand on words."

22   The martial arts, etc.

23   In *The Book of Five Rings*, the great swordsman Miyamoto Musashi states, "In this Way especially, if you misperceive it or become lost just a little, you will fall into distortion. You will not reach the essence of the martial arts by merely looking at this book... Rather, you should consider these principles as though they were discovered from your own mind, and continually make great efforts to make them a physical part of yourself."

24   *Kensho*: Lit., "seeing one's nature." At its deepest, this is making the discovery on one's own that the Buddha nature is within one's own mind. In Bodhidharma's *Sermon On Awakening to One's Nature*, he states, "Pointing directly at man's mind; see your own nature and become a Buddha. This is a special transmission beyond the scriptures, not standing on words or letters."

BIBLIOGRAPHY

Works in Japanese and Chinese

Amada Jirokichi, ed. *Zoku kendo shugi*. Tokyo: Tokyo Shoka Daigaku Kendobu, 1923.

Chigiri Kosai. *Tengu no kenkyu*. Tokyo: Hara Shobo, 2004

Chuang Wan-shou, ed. *Hsin I Lieh-tzu Tushu*. Taipei: Sanmin Shushu, 1994.

Fukunaga Mitsuji & Kozen Hiroshi, eds. *Roshi, Soshi*. Tokyo: Chikuma Shobo, 2004.

Fukunaga Takehiko, ed. *Konjaku monogatari*. Tokyo: Kawade Shobo Shinsha, 1976.

Hasegawa Tadashi, ed. *Taiheiki, Shinpen Nihon koten bungaku zenshu, Vol. 54*. Tokyo: Shogakukan, 1994.

Hayakawa Junzaburo, ed. *Bujutsu sosho*, Tokyo; Kokusho Kankokai, 1915

Ichikawa Hakugen, ed. *Nihon no zen goroku, Vol. 13*. Tokyo: Kodansha, 1978

Imai Usaburo, ed. *Saikontan*. Tokyo: Iwanami Shoten, 1982.

Kaku Kozo. *Miyamoto Musashi Jiten*. Tokyo: Tokyodo Shuppan, 2001.

Kanaya Osamu, ed. *Rongo*. Tokyo: Iwanami Shoten, 1963.

Kobayashi Nobuaki. *Resshi*. Tokyo: Meiji Shoin, 2004.

Kuramadera Kyomubu, *Kuramayama shoshi*. Kyoto: Seikosha, 1995

Nagata Bunshodo Henshubu, ed. *Kongo-kyo*. Tokyo: Nagata Bunshodo, 1956.

Nakano Mitsutoshi, ed. *Inaka soji, Tosei heta dangi, Tosei anasagashi*. Tokyo: Iwanami Shoten, 1990.

Ohashi Shin'ichi. *Otera mairi*. Tokyo: Tetsubunkan, 1932.

Saigusa Hiroto and Shimizu Ikutaro, ed. *Nihon tetsugaku shiso zensho*, Vol. 15. Tokyo: Heibonsha, 1980

Shimada Kenji, ed. *Daigaku, Chuyo*. Tokyo: Asahi Shinbunsha, 1967.

Shogaku Tosho, ed. *Koji kotowaza no jiten*. Tokyo: Shogakukan, 1986.

Yoshida Yutaka, ed. *Budo hidensho*. Tokyo: Tokuma Shoten, 1968.

Works in English

Blacker, Carmen. *The Catalpa Bow*. London: George Allen & Unwin Ltd., 1975.

Callicut, J. Baird & Ames, Roger T., eds. *Nature in Asian Traditions of Thought*. Albany: State Univ. of New York Press, 1989.

Chan, Wing-tsit. *A Source Book in Chinese Philosophy*. Princeton: Princeton University Press, 1963.

Frederic, Louis. *Buddhism*. Paris: Flammarion, 1995

Hori, Ichiro. *Folk Religion in Japan*. Chicago: The University of Chicago Press, 1968.

Issai Chozashi. *The Way of the Sword*. Translated from German edition (Die Kunst der Bergdämonen) of the original Japanese book *Tengu Geijutsuron* by Betty Fitzgerald.

Kammer, Reinhard, ed. *The Way of the Sword*. London: Arkana, 1986.

Miyake, Hitoshi. *Shugendo*. Ann Arbor: Center for Japanese Studies, University of Michigan, 2001.

Needham, Joseph. *Science and Civilization in China, Vol. 2*. Cambridge: Cambridge University Press, 1956.

——. *The Shorter Science and Civilization in China*. Cambridge: Cambridge University Press, 1978.

Skoss, Diane, ed. *Koryu Bujutsu: Classical Warrior Traditions of Japan*. Berkeley Heights: Koryu Books, 1997.

——, ed. *Sword and Spirit: Classical Warrior Traditions of Japan, Vol. 2*. Berkeley Heights: Koryu Books, 1999.

Sze, Mai-mai. *The Mustard Seed Garden Manual of Painting*. Princeton: Bollingen series, Princeton University Press, 1963.

Tanaka, Fumon. *Samurai Fighting Arts*. Tokyo: Kodansha International, 2003.

Tokitsu, Kenji. *Ki and the Way of the Martial Arts*. Boston: Shambala, 2003.

Vessantara. *The Mandala of the Five Buddhas*. Birmingham: Windhorse Press, 1999.

Wild Bird Society of Japan. *Birds of Japan*. Tokyo: Kodansha International, 1982

Wilson, William Scott, trans. *The Book of Five Rings*. Tokyo: Kodansha International, 2002.

——, trans. *The Roots of Wisdom: Saikontan*. Tokyo: Kodansha International, 1985.

——, trans. *The Unfettered Mind*. Tokyo: Kodansha Iinternational, 1986.

The family crest on the front jacket is a motif combining a military fan and bamboo leaves, and is somewhat reminiscent of tengu (demon), who are usually in possession of a fan. Above and on the back jacket is a crest with encircled hawk's feathers, the emblem of the Kuze family, which controlled the Sekiyado fief. Under his real name of Niwa Jurozaemon Tadaaki, Issai Chozanshi served as a samurai for the Kuze clan.

（英文版）天狗芸 術 論
The Demon's Sermon on the Martial Arts and Other Tales

2006 年 7 月 26 日　第 1 刷発行

著　者　　佚斎樗山子
訳　者　　ウィリアム・スコット・ウィルソン
発行者　　富田　充
発行所　　講談社インターナショナル株式会社
　　　　　〒 112-8652 東京都文京区音羽 1-17-14
　　　　　電話　03-3944-6493（編集部）
　　　　　　　　03-3944-6492（マーケティング部・業務部）
　　　　　ホームページ　www.kodansha-intl.com

印刷・製本所　大日本印刷株式会社